Make America Civil Again

The Transforming Power of Treating People Right

Wayne Wolf, Ph.D.

Make America Civil Again

The Transforming Power of Treating People Right

Wayne Wolf, Ph.D.

ELEVATION PRESS
OF COLORADO

Make America Civil Again
The Transforming Power of Treating People Right

by Wayne Wolf, Ph.D.

Copyright © 2025 by Wayne Wolf, Ph.D.

Cover and interior design and interior formatting by Donna Marie Benjamin of Elevation Press of Colorado.

The heart design appearing on the cover incorporates elements of the American flag. It is not intended to replicate any existing copyrighted image or logo. An internet image search reveals similar designs but no identical match. U.S. government databases which identify copyrighted images and logos include similar but not identical designs. The American flag itself is considered to be in the public domain and this book's cover design does not include any company name or company logo. Therefore, this design is determined to be unencumbered by pre-existing copyrights.

All rights reserved. No part of this publication may be reproduced, distributed, or transmitted in any form or by any means, including photocopying, recording, or other electronic or mechanical methods, without the prior written permission of the publisher, except in the case of brief quotations embodied in critical reviews and certain other non-commercial uses permitted by copyright law. For permission requests, write to the author at the address below:

Wayne Wolf
16841 Rimrock Road
Cedaredge, CO 81413

Ordering information: Quantity sales. Special discounts are available on quantity purchases by book clubs, corporations, associations, and others. For details, contact the publisher at the address above.

ISBN 978-0-932624-34-5

1. Main category — [Political Science] 2. Other categories — [Christianity]

Cedaredge, Colorado
www.elevation-press-books.com

A Vision of Civility

Civility is not about letting people run over us. Civility is not giving up or automatically giving in. Civility does not shun strong measures when they are necessary to protect life and liberty.

Civility believes the truth and seeks what is right before it seeks what is expedient. Civility balances freedom with responsibility. Civility uses resources wisely.

Civility invites participation. Civility is not arrogant or demeaning. Civility is considerate, patient, kind, just, merciful, and humble.

Civility overcomes evil with good. Civility wins people over by example. Civility treats others the way we would like to be treated.

Civility prays for God's kingdom to come and for His will to be done on earth as it is in heaven.

Table of Contents

Chapter 1
The Challenge of Incivility 1

Chapter 2
Is Walking with God a Help or Hindrance
to Civility? 17

Chapter 3
What Do I Know? 43

Chapter 4
The Political Spectrum 69

Chapter 5
Civil Leadership Matters 87

Chapter 6
Choice Choices for Big Ed 103

Chapter 7
A Calm Assessment of Socialism 121

Chapter 8
The Use of Law for Social Change 133

Chapter 9
The Political Climate 165

Chapter 10
The Importance of Local Government 187

Chapter 11
Election Integrity 209

Chapter 12
Heavenly Government 235

References 261

Chapter 1

The Challenge of Incivility

People say:

"I dread election time with all the negative ads."

"It does not stop on the second Tuesday in November. That Kavanaugh hearing was a travesty."

"With all the protests and the heated rhetoric, I am afraid we are headed for a civil war."

During the 2020 election, President Donald Trump said if Joe Biden was elected President, America would be destroyed. On January 6, 2021, a few hundred people violently breached the security on the west side of the Capitol building and attempted to delay the official report of state electors for President. Later, several hundred peaceful protesters were allowed to enter the east side of the Capitol only to be subsequently imprisoned despite some of them having permits to speak on the grounds.

In 2024, President Joe Biden said if Donald Trump was re-elected President, democracy would end. On July 13, candidate Trump was less than an inch from being killed by a would-be assassin's bullet.

Former Secretary of State Hillary Clinton said, "You cannot be civil with a party that wants to destroy what you stand for, what you care about" (Cummings, 2018).

Is incivility inevitable?

Not every Democrat agrees with Secretary Clinton's remark. Democratic Senator Heidi Heitkamp from North Dakota said, "I can't imagine how you get anything done if you don't bring civility back into politics, and that goes for both sides" (Phillips, 2018).

School principal and Democrat Barbara Condra wrote a book on *The Insanity of Incivility*. Condra is also a Christian, and I agree with her about how governing officials should conduct themselves. It is not by trying to win at all costs. "Woe to him who builds a city with bloodshed and establishes a town by crime" (Habakkuk 2:12 NIV).

Early in her student days, Hillary Clinton wrote a paper on Sal Alinsky and subsequently adopted many of his views. Alinsky (1989) said that the question of whether or not the end justifies the means is irrelevant. In his book *Rules for Radicals,* Alinsky said great leaders do whatever is necessary to accomplish a great goal. Then they come up with something to justify their action. Some politicians think that power is the most necessary tool to implement their goals.

Dick Cheney Right or Wrong

Dick Cheney is an example of a Republican who agreed with Clinton that civility is not practical. Cheney thought a key to American prosperity was a strong American presence in the Middle East. As Secretary of Defense under President George H. W. Bush, Dick Cheney was recognized as one of the heroes coming out of Desert Storm, the first Gulf War. The elder Bush's son, George W. Bush picked Cheney to be his Vice President. As Vice President, Cheney manipulated himself into a position of power where no one else in the administration could effectively challenge him.

After Cheney had been found to be right so many times early in his career, he may have become overconfident in his positions and not respectful enough of input from others. Cheney thought Sadam Hussein was actively supporting al Qaeda, that Ahmed Chalabi would be welcomed as a replacement for Hussein, and that Hussein had amassed huge stockpiles of material that could soon be used as Weapons of Mass Destruction against US interests. It turned out that Cheney was wrong on all three points, and it cost America dearly.

In the First Gulf War, other countries supported the United States. By comparison, some countries balked at the prospect of a second gulf war, whereupon Cheney advocated for the US to move forward quickly without them (Mann, 2020). Desert Storm (the First Gulf War) had cost some $60 billion, of which Kuwait and Saudi Arabia paid $32 billion. In one of the shortest wars in history, 154 American soldiers lost their lives. In contrast, by the tenth anniversary of the second invasion of Iraq, Desert Shield had cost the US $2.2 trillion (Brown University, 2013) and Desert Shield US service member fatalities were 4,488 plus 3400 contractors. Former President Bush grieved over their sacrifice.

Speaker of the House Newt Gingrich and his colleagues had worked hard with the Clinton Administration to have surplus budgets that reduced the national debt. Largely because of Desert Shield, the Bush administration submitted huge deficit budgets. Cheney said that Obama was the worst president in his lifetime. Obama replied that was interesting because he thought Cheney was the worst president in his.

When Cheney had to work with others, as he did in the First Gulf War, he did well. When he did not think he had to listen to others, as he advocated a second gulf war, he did not do well. When a person gains a reputation for being right and powerful, they are most vulnerable to being wrong and uncivil.

One way to respond to Secretary Clinton's uncivil approach is to match or surpass her incivility as Dick Cheney did. Another approach is to give in. Although Cheney was devious in slanting information from his office to the President, George W. Bush knew enough of what was going on that he could have stopped Cheney's war mongering, but he chose to give in. Some blame President George W. Bush for being too civil, but he was not being too civil because *giving in is not civil*. To believe that civility in any form was responsible for poor decisions is to embrace a misunderstanding of civility. It was not civil to give in to Cheney, nor was it civil to give in to the wealthy establishment who advocated for a trillion-dollar bail-out. (At the time, a trillion dollars was a lot of money.) Historians have not been kind to Nevel Chamberlin for repeatedly giving in to Hitler and at the same time have given credit to Winston Churchill for his bulldog determination not to give in to Hitler or Stalin.

Giving up on a worthy cause is not civil either. Some are giving up on the abortion issue because the abortionists have been able to push their deceptive arguments. Progress has been slow and not what those who oppose abortion would like it to be. Nevertheless, it is the persistent who generally win out in the long (long, long) run. Giving in is only civil when it is strategic to make a victory possible, such as the British evacuation from Dunkirk.

In response to Secretary Clinton's call for her side to disregard civility, we on the other side can do better. We can make civility work for us. During the Cold War, President Kennedy (1961) said, "Civility is not a sign of weakness…Let us never negotiate out of fear, but let us never fear to negotiate." Some current Democrats and Republicans are more afraid of negotiating with each other than Kennedy was of negotiating with Khrushchev in the 1960s.

A Local Experience in Civility

As a Delta County Commissioner in Western Colorado, I was privileged to be Co-Chairman of a local Public Lands Partnership which included stakeholder representatives from ranching, recreation, business, local elected officials, state wildlife experts, and federal land managers. We primarily worked on increasing wildlife habitat and reducing wildfire fuels on the Uncompahgre Plateau. We also worked on preventing the spread of Spruce Beetle infestation on the Grand Mesa. We spent much time on the ground so that we were discussing what each of us actually witnessed rather than letting our political ideologies dictate our agenda.

Using active management plans, we worked together to develop a variety of vegetation with patches in differing stages of maturity. Increased native vegetation has allowed the Colorado Division of Wildlife to manage a larger deer population while also supporting local ranchers. The Deputy Secretary of the Interior gave our Public Lands Partnership an award for our exemplary collaboration, which transformed areas susceptible to catastrophic wildfire into prime wildlife habitat. None of our accomplishments would have been possible if any one of us had insisted on doing things our own way without regard for other interests.

Consider the Constitution

One of the greatest protections against incivility is the United States Constitution, which was drafted by patriots who were intent on making it as difficult as possible for any one individual to unnecessarily restrict the freedom of others. The Constitution elaborated on the concepts presented in the Declaration of Independence that rights originate from God and not men. In the 1700s the

British government claimed unlimited power. American colonists maintained that human government is limited in power. John Quincy Adams (1837) said, "A moral Ruler of the universe, the Governor and Controller of all human power is the only unlimited sovereign acknowledged by the Declaration of Independence." The mantra for many in the War for American Independence was, "No king but Jesus."

Reporters asked President Trump if he would be a dictator. They apparently did not understand that becoming a dictator was not his decision to make. Over two hundred years ago Americans shed their blood in order to have a government where the power of the national executive is checked. Acting as a whole, Congress has more power than any one man. In the 1930s, the Nazis gained control of the Reichstag and then gave unchecked power to Hitler. It is not that simple in the US. Even when the Democrats or Republicans control both Houses of Congress and the Presidency, they cannot wield unlimited power. The party in power must still deal with the minority in the Senate as well as the Supreme Court, Governors, other state officials, and tens of thousands serving in local jurisdictions. It is up to each American individual whether they want to cede their power to a president. It is also the choice of every American whether or not to give in to pressure to follow immoral leadership. It is up to each individual in America whether or not to exercise the right to a government of, by, and for the people.

Common Sense

In the 1700s, Americans grew to detest encroachments by King George III into their rights as Englishmen. In 1776, Thomas Paine took things further in a pamphlet entitled *Common Sense* in which he argued against having any human king at all, anywhere. At first, many Americans were emotionally opposed to Paine but soon they came around to his way of thinking. In his brief survey of history, Paine pointed out that most of the time single leadership had resulted in encroachments into the freedom of its constituents. Although Paine was probably not a theologically conservative

Christian, he was definitely a political conservative who began his arguments against kingship with a couple of passages from the Bible.

In particular, Paine cited Judges 8:22-23 which says "Then the men of Israel said to Gideon, 'Rule over us, both you and your son, also your son's son, for you have delivered us from the hand of Midian' But Gideon said to them, 'I will not rule over you, nor shall my son rule over you; the LORD shall rule over you." Paine not only opposed kingship but, with equal veracity, he ridiculed the idea of rule being inherited. The children of a king are often the least fit for leadership. As Americans rejected the idea of inherited sovereignty, they embraced elections for choosing leaders.

Paine also pointed to 1 Samuel 8 where the elders of Israel told Samuel that they wanted a king to judge them like all the other nations. God sent Samuel to warn the people about the ways of a king. Such an absolute ruler would take their sons and make them warriors. He would take their daughters for perfumers and cooks and bakers. He would take the best of their fields and their vineyards and their olive groves. He would take their flocks and they themselves would become his servants.

Nevertheless, the people refused to listen to Samuel and insisted that, like other nations, they have a king who would go before them to fight their battles. In general, people are willing to pay dearly in order to have someone else fight their battles for them. Not so the early Americans. They fought for their freedom rather than submit to one who would take their property.

An American Framework

The American founders put together a framework for separation of powers that has served us well in protecting us from dictator tyranny. This framework has allowed Americans to organize their government and outperform oppressive collectivist nations. A major reason Americans have been prosperous is because of our decentralized system of government. Most power has been kept at the local level, where decisions can be made efficiently.

For example, questions about the location of roads and utilities need to be decided locally rather than being sent to a central government which would be overwhelmed by the process of making myriads of local decisions. Keeping leadership diversified can help limit bad decisions.

When I was sworn in as a county commissioner, I pledged to support and defend the US Constitution. As I and tens of thousands of other elected officials take care of our responsibilities, we truly have a government by the people and not one man—not even a man as unselfish as George Washington.

George Washington was noted for getting things done during terrible strife. One of the works that reflects his philosophy is a treatise on civility that he put together as a teen based on a work by French Jesuits. It is now called George Washington's Rules of Civility and Decent Behavior in Company and Conversation. Of his 110 rules, Number 12 states:

"Shake not the head, Feet, or Legs roll not the Eyes lift not one eyebrow higher than the other wry not the mouth, and bedew no man's face with your Spittle, by approaching to near him when you Speak."

This is just one example of courteous behaviors which show concern for others. Such behaviors are also practical. Since the arrival of COVID, the commitment not to get spittle on someone else's face is particularly relevant.

In his last address to Congress, Washington prayed that God would "most graciously be pleased to dispose to us all to do justice, to love mercy, and to demean ourselves with that charity, humility, and specific temper of the mind which were the characteristics of the Divine Author." His listeners at that time would have recognized Washington's sentiments as mirroring the Old Testament, Micah 6:8, "He has shown you, O man, what is good; and what does the Lord require of you but to do justly, to love mercy, and to walk humbly with your God?" (KJV).

When Washington referred to humility as a charity, he was saying it is a gift from God. From his teen years into his senior years,

Washington sought to put humility into practice. A right understanding of ourselves and of our Divine Author is the essential basis for civility. The American founders recognized the Lord Jesus Christ as the most perfect example of how leaders should conduct themselves.

Civility encompasses a myriad of behaviors from not bedewing someone's face to opposing tyranny an ocean away. Stated positively, civility is loving your neighbor and treating them as well as you would like to be treated.

In contrast to Washington's prayer for Biblical humility, other people have said that religion, and Christianity in particular, has contributed more to incivility than any other factor. Such a position suppresses our best hope for civility and therefore should be challenged.

Chapter 2

Is Walking with God a Help or Hindrance to Civility?

People on the political left, in general, think their purpose in life is to gain concessions from the "haves" in order to make life better for the "have-nots." They believe the rich got wealthy at the expense of the poor. Many, not all, who have this view think that the Christian religion is the biggest rip-off of all. From the Crusaders harassing Muslims to the superstitious executions in the Salem Witch Trials, along with the Inquisition, some think that religious people have committed the greatest atrocities in human history. Therefore, such doubters maintain that the path to civil governance is to disregard, even reject religion.

The history of Christians not being very Christian is an embarrassment and when these things are brought up, we tend to go away with our heads hanging. I would like to put atrocities of the Christian religious in perspective and then make a distinction between Christianity the religion and walking with God in relationship.

The Need for Context

The Salem Witch Trials, Crusades, and Inquisition are aberrations in need of context. While I was visiting a friend, another person's name came up. I had just had an encounter with that person and figured I would talk about it.

For a moment, I thought I shouldn't tell that story.

"Why not?" I asked myself. "Afterall, it happened."

As soon as I told the story, I had one of the worst burdens of guilt that I have ever experienced. Every item in my story was true. The problem was that the story reflected badly on that individual. The story was not representative of that person's generally fine character, so I considered that repeating the story was a case of bearing false witness about him.

It is not that the Salem Witch Trials did not happen, but they are exceptions. They do not accurately reflect colonial Christianity. America's Ivy League colleges were founded by Christian leaders who were most interested in dispelling superstition and advancing our understanding of reality. They were particularly interested in prudent governance, both ecclesiastical (church) and civil (state) in which people would be assured of due process and just judgements. Decent and orderly churchgoers were the majority in New England from the landing of the Pilgrims in 1620 through the Declaration of Independence in 1776. Although there were scattered minor incidences of witch accusations, the Salem Witch Trials involved one church in one county from February 1692 to May 1693 (Smithsonian, 2022). That was less than a year and a half.

Stretching it out to characterize Christianity in the colonies for 156 years (1620–1776) is a false witness. Such a sweeping generalization is also an incivility.

Depravity by the Numbers

Is the Christian religion the greatest scourge on humanity? It is estimated that some million and a half people died in the Crusades. Most of those fatalities were Christians who died on the grueling trip from Europe to the Holy Land. Less than half a million Muslims died, and they were not martyrs; they died in battle while protecting property that their ancestors had taken from others, including Christians.

In two centuries, the Spanish Inquisition put some 32,000 people to death. Communist dictators are responsible for the deaths of some 110 million people. Hitler was responsible for the deaths of some 20 million Jews and Poles (Rummel, 1993). Members of the Christian religion have killed far fewer than atheistic/agnostic leaders have. Even if you add deaths from battles between Protestant states and Catholic states, it could be argued that atheism is more than fifty times worse if the number of killing others is the standard. Compare some 2 million killed by Christian actions to more than 130 million who died at the hands of atheistic/agnostic leaders.

Billy Graham called his gatherings crusades, stating that he purposely chose the word to redeem it. According to his website, Billy Graham spoke to more than 178 million people—considerably more than the number killed by atheistic dictators. In his crusades, Billy Graham used persuasion, not force. He believed that acceptance of the Good News he preached would change lives for the better both now and in eternity. Billy Graham's message explained what it means to walk with God. It begins with the bad news that there are consequences for going our own way—away from God. Individual sins are evidence of the condition of our heart, which is in sinful rebellion. Jesus provides freedom from the burden of sin so that we can walk in relationship with Him.

The Abuses of the Inquisition Addressed

People who walk with God were victims of the European Inquisition—not its perpetrators. The Inquisitors were religious people who did not let the Bible be their guide. Inquisitors forced the accused to testify against themselves. Those who would not confess were tortured and executed. They were not allowed to face their accusers, which facilitated false accusations. Supporting witnesses were often too afraid to speak. The accused had no representation. Suspects generally were not told what charges were being brought against them. Commonly, the only people present were the accused, a scribe, and the inquisitor. Execution was often by burning at the stake. Their property was taken by those favored by the religious persecutors. (History.com Editors, 2018).

The American founders were very much aware of the abuses of the Inquisitors and thus they placed provisions in the Constitution to prevent such atrocities from occurring in the

United States. They designed a government that distributed power so that officials could be challenged, and specific provisions were made to protect individuals, such as, the Sixth Amendment to the US Constitution:

> "In all criminal prosecutions, the accused shall enjoy the right to a speedy and public trial, by an impartial jury of the State and district wherein the crime shall have been committed, which district shall have been previously ascertained by law, and to be informed of the nature and cause of the accusation; to be confronted with the witnesses against him; to have compulsory process for obtaining witnesses in his favor, and to have the Assistance of Counsel for his defense" (National Archives, 1789).

The provision for trial in the locality of the alleged crime was because King George was notorious for transporting colonists across the sea to stand trial in England for pretended offenses (Declaration of Independence, 1776). Other grievances against King George laid out in the Declaration of Independence included lodging large bodies of armed troops in colonists' homes, and depriving colonists of trial by jury. Furthermore, "cruel and unusual punishments were prohibited by the eighth amendment" (National Archives, 1789).

The Constitution's First Amendment includes a right to petition the government for a redress of grievances. King George III had ignored the colonists' repeated petitions for redress against his oppressions. The Third Amendment to the Constitution limits the quartering of soldiers without the consent of the house owner. The Fifth Amendment, among other provisions, prohibits a person from being forced to be a witness against himself.

The actions of the Inquisitors were the opposite of mercy. Therefore, the American founders' efforts to stop tyranny could be viewed as merciful. Justice and mercy are not opposites. They are complimentary. Both justice and mercy are opposites of tyranny. God's admonition to seek mercy and justice are therefore calls to oppose tyranny. It is easiest to oppose tyranny before it becomes established.

The Presence or Absence of Violence

We often think of civility in terms of the amount of violence which is present or absent. However, civility is not primarily a matter of the degree of violence involved but rather the appropriateness of whatever action is taken. The early Americans felt they needed to justify violence in their struggles with Great Britain because violence is the exception and not the rule of civility. While the theme of this book is the importance and effectiveness of peaceful civility, I will take a few pages here to painfully address civil violence. One of the arguments that many pastors used to persuade reluctant Christians to participate in the War for Independence was by using ancient Israel's dealing with tyrants as an example. On May 29,

1776, Samuel West, a pastor at Dartmouth, addressed the Massachusetts Bay House of Representatives with a sermon on the proper response to the tyranny of Jabin, King of Canaan, with implications concerning King George III of Briton (Byrd, 2017).

The people of Israel cried out to God to deliver them from Jabin's cruelty. Jabin's barbarous General Sisera and his troops were routed by the Israelites (Judges 4). Exhausted, Sisera entered the tent of Jael and, relying on the peace which existed between King Jabin and the household of Jael and her husband, he went to sleep. Then Jael drove a tent peg through Sisera's temple into the ground.

That is indeed gory, but before we get too judgmental may we ask, "Is it not also gory to poke a hole in an unborn baby's head and suck out the infant's brains?"

Can one act of violence be justified and another condemned?

Yes, we can. Sisera had inflicted pain and suffering on others. He was proficient in killing. He had chosen to be a soldier with the accompanying risk of death. In contrast, an unborn baby is innocent and deserving of protection. Right and wrong can be legitimately differentiated.

The emphasis of West's sermon came from *The Song of Deborah* found in the fifth chapter of Judges. In praising God for delivering Israel from Sisera by the hand of Jael, Deborah adds a curse on the people of Meroz because they did not come to help the Lord against the mighty (Judges 5:23). West was adamant in his condemnation of those who would not help the patriots to defeat the bloody British. Defeating the British was crucial at that time because "tyranny and arbitrary power are utterly inconsistent and subversive of justice" (Byrd, 2017).

The support of hundreds of pastors for the War of Independence was greatly influential. Following is a small sampling of sermons used to justify killing British soldiers:

John Lathrop, *Innocent Blood Crying to God from the Streets of Boston.*

Jonas Clark, *The fate of Blood-thirsty Oppressors, and God's Tender Care of his Distressed.*

Samuel Langdon, *The Republic of the Israelites an Example to the American States.*

Samuel Finley, *The Danger of Neutrality, in the Cause of God, and our Country.*

Nathaniel Whitaker, *The Antidote Against Toryism. Or the Curse of Meroz.*

Sylvanus Conant, *The Art of War, the Gift of God.*

The Roots of Democracy

Like many others, I was taught the negative aspects of the history of Christianity, but not the positive. For example, I heard that American governance was inspired by the Greeks. I heard nothing about the influence of faith on the founders of the United States of America. The Greek philosophers did spend time discussing governance. Coming from the Greek language are the words monarchy (one rule), aristocracy (privileged rule), oligarchy (rule by the few), and democracy (people rule). The word tyranny is also of Greek derivation.

Having heard in my undergraduate studies that America is a democracy inspired by the Greeks, I was surprised to learn in my doctoral studies that Plato, who wrote *The Republic,* was one of the most anti-democratic of philosophers. Mobocracy (democracy) had killed his mentor, Socrates. In specific reference to Aristotle, Thomas Jefferson said that little edification came from the Greek writings. While they idealized the value of personal liberty, they contributed nothing to the development of a government best calculated to preserve that liberty (Jefferson, 1816). They vacillated between tyrannical mobs and tyrannical dictators. *The Federalist Number 55* (1788) says, "Had every Athenian citizen been a Socrates, every Athenian assembly would still have been a mob."

According to Jefferson, Representative Democracy was the invention of the American mind (Jefferson, 1816). The American mind included the co-development of church and state structures that maximized citizen input into governance while protecting liberties for individuals from potentially misguided majorities. The American mindset was greatly influenced by the Great Awakening of the 1730s, which called on people as individuals to establish a relationship with God and live moral lives (Drayer, 2016). New Light preachers, who were essential in fostering the Great Awakening, inspired believers to rediscover the teaching of the Apostle Paul, "There is neither Jew nor Greek, slave nor free men, there is neither male nor female; for you are all one in Christ Jesus" (Galatians 3:28). In the new churches, people who had been labeled as commoners were elected to be leaders. The New Lights developed into today's Evangelicals.

According to David Barton, the American founders quoted the Bible more than any other book. The second most quoted works were from British philosopher John Locke who was a Christian who thoughtfully discussed the necessity of civility in governance. The secular economists who rewrote American history do not give John Locke his proper due just as they ignore the crucial positive aspects of Christian influence and greatly magnify the negatives. Colonial history is Greek to leftists.

True Life Church

Around the year 2000, my wife Kristine, our son Brian, and I started going to True Life Church in Cedaredge, Colorado. In a mutual interview process, I asked why True Life did not have monthly business meetings. Pastor Bob Hillyer answered with a question, "Have you ever been to a church business meeting?"

Having been a member of Baptist churches since I was 14, I had participated in scores of them. They were mostly run according to *Robert's Rules of Order,* which was written by a businessman who was the son of a Baptist preacher. I did not personally see a problem with the democratic, majority rule process of conducting church meetings. But I came to suspect that one of the reasons there are so many Baptist churches is because of blow-ups over issues that appear minor to outsiders.

True Life Church is governed by a board of deacons who serve three-year terms. The deacons are elected at annual business meetings.

This representative governance seems to work well in keeping the congregation focused on major issues instead of getting bogged down in trivial ones.

The concept of *presbyters* (members of a church governing body) is the source of the idea of representation in civil governance. Many American churches which are not of the Presbyterian denomination have a presbyterian form of governance. America's founders developed, as a key element of a republic, a Representative Democracy based on Presbyterian/Baptist principles with emphasis on representation. James Madison (1787) said that representation is what defines a republic.

The influence of a Biblical worldview on the American republic is represented by quotes compiled by David Barton (2008):

"The Bible contains the most profound Philosophy, the most perfect Morality, and the most refined Policy that was ever conceived upon Earth" (John Adams, 1804, Second U.S. President).

"By conveying the Bible to people...we certainly do them a most interesting act of kindness" (John Jay, 1824, Original Chief Justice of the Supreme Court).

"The moral principles and precepts found in the Scriptures ought to form the basis of all our civil constitution and laws" (Noah Webster, 1832, "Schoolmaster to America").

"The Declaration of Independence laid the cornerstone of human government upon the first precepts of Christianity" (John Quincy Adams, 1837, Sixth U.S. President).

The Doctrine of Sin

With such a substantial influence of church people on American government, why do many secular professors take shots at Biblical ideas? One of the reasons that some people do not like Christianity is because of the doctrine of sin. It hurts our pride to think that there is something wrong with us. I was 14 when my parents started taking our family to church. I remember feeling uncomfortable when the preacher talked about sin. Evangelicals call it being under conviction. No one likes being under conviction and we generally try to get out of it.

There are two ways to get out of conviction. One is to accept the truth that we have sinned and the truth that Jesus is the Savior. The alternative plan is to rid oneself of anyone and anything that elicits feelings of guilt, for example, Christians. In the extreme, leftist strategy has been to restrict the freedom of Christians in an effort to isolate them so they cannot irritate or infect others. If people were a little more open-minded, they would realize that calling attention to wrong behavior can lead to an improving society that is truly progressive.

After living in a dorm for a month, my Student Assistant, Bill, drew me aside and said, "How are you and John getting along?"

"Okay," I said.

"Well, John doesn't think so," Bill said. "There's another 'God-squader' down at the end of the hall. You can move in with him and his roommate will move in with John so they can enjoy their partying."

I took this advice and Keith turned out to be a great roommate, but the idea that John wanted a different roommate stung a little. I was trying to get along. I had the only TV on the floor and in retrospect I think the final straw for John was when he came in one evening to find me watching a Billy Graham crusade.

It is often claimed that Christians are judgmental and do not want to be around sinners. I have found it also true that some sinners do not want Christians around. On Facebook, I challenged a former teacher colleague of mine on his abortion postings, and he unfriended me.

If we got rid of the doctrine of sin, many people would not have a problem with Christians. I think that is why liberals minimize sin. Conservative Christians do not minimize sin, although we might get hung up focusing on particular sins and over-looking others.

What does this talk about sin have to do with governance? The nature of governed individuals is a fundamental issue in the design of government. If people are malleable groups driven by needs, then gaining power to shape their environment is the pathway to progressive social change. However, if the pathway to social change is through individuals becoming right with God, then the role of government becomes the protector of the individual's right to share the Gospel, rather than passing legislation to try to control people.

The Christian doctrine of sin that we have fallen short of our potential has a profound meaning. It means that everyone has great potential. Our founders were aware of both the negative and positive implications of sin. They designed a government that maximized our potential for good while reducing the possibility that an evil ruler could wreak havoc over the whole society. The separation of powers was motivated by a desire to reduce the prospect for tyranny. In basic studies of American governance, we learn about the separation of powers to carry out the functions of government: legislative, executive, and judicial. Less emphasized generally, but just as important, is the separation of governmental functions into local, state, and national entities. I have made this point before and will repeat it later because this further separation of governmental functions is a key to increasing civility.

Church and State

During the development of church governments and state governments in early America, there was also a maturing of the distinct roles each should maintain in society. Isaac Baucus was a Baptist pastor who was a leader in the movement to keep civil government out of church business. For example, he opposed governmental taxation for the purpose of paying pastors' salaries. The practical reason for this was because he did not want Baptists to be taxed to pay for Congregationalist pastors in addition to supporting their own clergy. Baucus was a strong ally of Madison and Jefferson in the development of the First Amendment.

Upon the election of Jefferson as President, the Baptist Association of Danbury, Connecticut, wrote a letter to him expressing their affectionate support. They reminded him that "Our sentiments are uniformly on the side of religious liberty that Religion is at all times and places a matter between God and individuals, that no man ought to suffer in name, person, effects on account of his religious opinions." In President Jefferson's famous letter of reply, he thanked them for their prayers for him, and said he also was praying for them. He expressed his affection for them and respect for their position. He did not say that the church should stay out of civil matters. Rather, he pledged to establish a "wall of separation of church and state" to keep the civil government out of church business. He did not propose to keep believers from expressing political views, as many have been deceived into thinking. If Jefferson's purpose was to shut Christianity out of government, then why did he use state funds to publish the words of Jesus for missionaries to share with Native Americans?

In this chapter, I have disputed the idea that an increased Christian influence would lead to pervasive witch trials, military crusades, and injustice. I have pointed out that religious Christians have a better track record of leadership than atheists. Better yet, I have emphasized that those who sought to walk with God have had a tremendously positive influence on civil governance. Faithful Christians seek a deeper relationship with God through Jesus Christ. Faithful Christians do not seek power to dictate how people should live and what they should believe. Such devoted Christians desire the freedom to voluntarily follow their understanding of biblical applications for their daily lives. Like myself, they desire to walk in relationship with God. Billy Graham's influential ministry has provided an example of the Christian methodology of evangelism. Loving persuasion is the goal of the conservative Christian, not force.

When the early Americans spoke about religion, they were generally referring to Christian beliefs. In that sense, religion is a good thing. However, when I think of religion in a more negative sense, I am generally thinking of Pharisaical rituals (narrow practices of the Pharisees) that enable a person to look pious on the outside, while being just as vile on the inside as a pagan. Jesus was tough on the Pharisees. A literal translation of the word for *hypocrite* is *actor*. Through all their pious acts, the Pharisees pretended that they were being obedient to God to gain admiration from men.

The real deal is for a person to be obedient to God in actuality. The crucial part of obeying God is to submit to His provision for our salvation, who is Jesus Christ. The indwelling Spirit of Christ enables us to be obedient in all other matters. Jesus says, in John 15, that He is the vine, the saved are the branches; without Him we can do nothing. Paul says, with God all things are possible—including civility. My first pastor said that we should be careful not to be overly enamored with men. He had a rough experience of being let down by a mentor whom he greatly admired. When people try to bring us down out of envy or other sinful motives, it can be tough to deal with, and it requires conscious restraint not to harm those who wish us ill.

Forgiveness

During the time I was running for state senate, a man wrote a letter about me and distributed it to newspapers throughout the district. His letter alleged that I did not uphold the Constitution or defend property rights. It was probably not the only reason I lost that election, but it certainly did not help. This was a low blow since I have always been a strong defender of people being able to use their property to the greatest reasonable extent. This man lived in a location which was on our way to Cedaredge. Whenever we drove by, Kristine and I got in the habit of praying for positive outcomes for him. One day, this man and I happened to meet at Sam's Club, and we had a good conversation in which I was able to convey that I only wished him the best.

As I humbly submit myself to Jesus, God gives me an inner peace that contributes to my being at peace with others. Jesus is the way to civility. Whether forgiving those who trespass against us or being careful not to bedew someone's face with spittle, God helps us to know what we should do as we walk humbly with Him. Until we know the truth, we cannot be free to be civil.

Chapter 3

What Do I Know?

The greatest incivility is to try to force someone to think our way, whereas the greatest civility is to kindly try to persuade someone to accept truth. The fundamental issue regarding civility is respect for being truthful. The political philosopher Machiavelli in *The Prince* (1532) said that the appearance of benevolence is beneficial, but being deceptive and ruthless are more important to being a successful leader. In his *Rules for Radicals* (1971), Saul Alinsky expressed similar extreme ideas. If there is no truth, it follows that there is no foundation for morality, which implies that there is no solid reason not to follow the teachings of Machiavelli and Alinsky. But truth and reason do exist, and civility will not return until our society embraces reason as the respected means to resolve conflict and make progress. As counterintuitive as it may seem, civility requires the ability to recognize that some teaching is wrong.

When I was a youngster, older people would greet each other with the question, "What do you know for sure?" Since many claim that no one can know anything for certain, that greeting should logically lead to silence, but it does not. People commonly claim that any one person's opinion is just as good as any other opinion. The criterion for acceptance of political views is no longer the reasonableness of a view, but rather the extent to which a view achieves popularity. Politics is now dominated by sales pitches that may or may not be grounded in reality.

An example of careful reasoning, German physicist Werner Heisenberg delivered lectures in 1927 at the University of Chicago on the principles of Quantum Theory (Heisenberg, 1930). Through several proofs Heisenberg conclusively demonstrated that we cannot know, simultaneously and with perfect accuracy, both the position and speed of a particle such as a photon or electron. This is popularly called the uncertainty principle. Indeed, there are things we cannot know for certain, but it is a gross misunderstanding of Heisenberg to claim that we cannot know anything for certain. If we cannot know anything for certain, how can we accept anything Heisenberg said, no matter how reasonable.

In Defense of Reasonably Held Knowledge

Please join me as I journey back to a time when I experienced reasonably held knowledge.

To give my mom a break, my grandpa would take me and my siblings with him to build barbed wire fences. He had a special hammer that was just the right weight for pounding staples. Its claw was just the right size for grasping a barb so that, using the right technique, you could pull wire tightly around a post. It was also good for digging dirt. One time as we were packing up to leave, Grandpa asked, "Wayne, where is my hammer?"

The prospect that the hammer was lost made me shake with fear. I quickly searched near one of my dirt projects and my fear was calmed, "Here's your hammer, Grandpa!" Sixty-plus years later I can tell you the exact location of that incident because it happened at the boundary where our old ranch adjoined two other properties on section and half-section lines. I could find the latitude and longitude for it. I still know where that hammer is too. It is on his saddle, which hangs in my shed, inside the pouch that he had specially made for it at Western Saddlery Company in Denver. As the Greek philosophers would say either "a" or "non-a" is true. Either the hammer was lost, or it was not. Sound knowledge can be built on that type of proposition. If things like hammers exist, and we have words for them, then a world full of reality becomes open for discussion.

Our experiences can be used as a springboard for conversation. Regarding my hammer story, most people live in the city so they might not relate to a barbed wire boundary fence to keep cattle in a pasture. Yet they probably could relate to a grandpa, a hammer, or fear.

John Godfrey Saxe's (1873) poem about the blind men and the elephant is used to illustrate the uncertainty doctrine. One man who felt the elephant's leg said the elephant was like a tree, one who bumped into the elephant's side said the elephant was like a wall, and one who felt its tail said the elephant was like a rope. To me, this story illustrates the possibility that, if people will listen to the observations of others, they can put together a better understanding of the world. I tend to view each encounter I have with others as an opportunity to refine my understanding of the elephant.

About Trees

As we discuss our encounters with our environment and each other we can build a substantial knowledge of individual and corporate reality. How can anyone seriously argue that there are no such things as trees or that we cannot know for sure when we experience them? I grew up on the edge of the Black Forest northeast of Colorado Springs. I can bring to mind several individual Ponderosa pine trees as well as images of interspersed meadows and woods.

The lower two-thirds of a particular 60-foot Ponderosa only contained a few short branches. Intent on climbing, I carefully tugged each branch in turn to see if it would support my two feet and one hand while I reached up to test the next. I hugged the rough black bark with my chest and legs, while smelling the tree's turpentine-like aroma and trying to avoid the sticky resin. A breeze stirred and just as I reached the top, I looked down and waved to my mom who had come outside. If she was impressed, she did not show it. Such anger and fear in her voice I never experienced at any other time as she told me to get down *CAREFULLY*. Can you imagine that my mother thought danger was not real?

(During this endeavor, I was a tree-hugger, however I generally don't get upset if a tree falls in the forest, whether I see it happen or not.)

Regardless of whether my mom or anyone else saw me climb that tree, I, in fact, climbed the tree. Our log house was made of local trees. This was true whether anyone outside the family saw Dad cut down the trees. To cite another example of tree reality, no one I know saw hundreds of spruce trees fall near the lofty Craig Crest Trail on Grand Mesa in Western Colorado, but many hikers see them lying on the ground and do not doubt that they fell. It is a part of our knowledge along with numerous other observations. When we conclude that trees fall, we are using inductive reasoning. Inductive reasoning is applied to establish, as fact, events that happen repeatedly.

Another example of inductive reasoning is based on my observation that it has snowed on Grand Mesa every year that I have lived near Cedaredge, Colorado. By observation and inductive reasoning, it is a fact that it snows every winter on Grand Mesa. Inductive reasoning moves from general observations to facts. Deductive reasoning moves from facts to specific actions. By deductive reasoning, I can say that it is probably going to snow on Grand Mesa this coming winter. After observing repeated phenomenon, humans use inductive reasoning to make conclusions, and we also use deductive reasoning which influences our actions. If someone told me that they had just driven over Grand Mesa and it was snowing hard, I could picture that experience. The worst white-out I ever endured was on the Mesa. So, because of that knowledge, when I hear of such conditions up there, I avoid the Mesa and drive through the lower valleys where it is not snowing.

Building a Common Knowledge Base

We can use experiences, observation, and reasoning to build a common knowledge base upon which we can make reasonable political decisions. For example, county officials in northern states make decisions about the level of snow plowing that will be done. A prudent decision will consider the amount of snow an area receives, the needs of constituents to safely travel, and the amount of funds available. As a county road supervisor, I made sure the roads were plowed before the school buses ran.

Whether or not we can have knowledge of reality is a crucial issue, but it is not difficult to solve. Abraham Lincoln liked to ask, "If you call a dog's tail a leg, how many legs does a dog have?" Then he would answer, "Four, because calling a dog's tail a leg doesn't make it one." Reality exists whether we believe it or not. Perception exists whether it matches reality or not. In the past, being out of touch with reality was labeled a psychological disorder. Now, in many circles, the abnormal is considered normal or progressive.

I have a passion for truth in a world that has a passion for appearance. Some of our ancestors decided to get married and head west. There was almost no courtship; a couple went to the Justice of the Peace and then stayed married for fifty years. Today, couples live together first, then spend thousands of dollars on a spectacular wedding to which every acquaintance and their uncle is invited, only to get divorced a few years later.

To Tell the Truth

One of the first non-ranch jobs I had was working as a janitorial supply salesman for a man named Joe. Joe would tell a potential customer one thing and tell me something else, so I knew he was not telling the truth—at least part of the time. Soon, I figured out that what he told me did not often match reality. I came to think that Joe had a different understanding of truth than the people I had grown up with. He would often say, "To tell you the truth." What that eventually meant to me was

I needed to watch out for what he said next. I needed to be cautious because whatever he said was just what he *wanted me to think* rather than any attempt on his part to match his statements with reality. At one time I thought what I viewed as the "Joe's School of Pretense" was isolated, but now I think it is widespread.

Before people in America *went truth numb,* two of the things we could agree on were that: 1) There is such a thing as the common good and 2) We do not perfectly agree on what that common good is. As a result of these agreements, it followed that American politics should be all about discussion and compromise to reach the best solution possible and then to keep working on making policy that benefits everyone to the greatest extent possible. To this ideal approach, I will add my own personal caveat. During my time as a county commissioner, I also had a principle of not harming anyone. For me it was not good enough to just benefit the majority. Policy also had to do no harm to anyone. We made the principle of harming no one work in Delta County. Perhaps this harm-no-one approach cannot be applied so well on a national level, but it could be applied more often than it is.

An example of disregarding the harm caused to some at the national level concerns the Little Sisters of the Poor. Many of us were upset that the Little Sisters of the Poor were required to participate in the "affordable" health care program that included birth control. Because of their convictions, the Sisters did not want and did not need that program. This is an example of the left's in-your-face attitude toward Christians. Liberals claim that conservatives are divisive. And yet, they ignore the fact that policies like forcing the Little Sisters to participate in the Affordable Care Act irritates conservatives greatly and drives us in large numbers to support people like President Trump. The practice of advocating for excessive government is the more fundamental cause of division than is the resistance to excessive government.

Guess Who Said It

Sometimes differences like the Little Sisters' issue sow division but sometimes political opponents are not as different as it may appear. To confront real issues, we need to evaluate what people actually say, rather than what other people say they said.

Guess who wrote the following quotes in his 2020 book. A hint: you will not hear his name associated with the concepts he states here on Fox News, talk radio, CNN, or MSNBC. As you consider these quotations, ask yourself: would it be possible to work with this person on policy that would benefit Americans? Here is the first quote:

> "And yet the pride in being American, the notion that America was the greatest country on earth—that was always a given. As a young man, I chafed against books that dismissed the notion of American exceptionalism; got into long, drawn-out arguments with friends

who insisted the American hegemon (America's dominant influence) was the root of oppression worldwide. I had lived overseas; I knew too much. That America fell perpetually short of its ideals, I readily conceded.... But the idea of America, the promise of America: this I clung to with a stubbornness that surprised even me. 'We hold these truths to be self-evident, that all men are created equal' that was my America."

Some might question whether this person was being truthful or if he just did not want his legacy to suggest that he was embarrassed to be an American. In either case, it opens a door for productive discussion. Truly listening requires some discernment. Later in the same book this politician wrote:

"I told myself then—and I like to tell myself still—that I left organizing because I saw the work I was doing as too slow, too limited, not able to match the needs of the people I hoped to serve. A local job-training center couldn't make up for thousands of steel jobs lost by a plant closing. An after-school program couldn't compensate for chronically underfunded schools, or kids raised by their grandparents because both parents were doing time. On every issue, it seemed, we kept bumping up against somebody—a politician, a bureaucrat, some distant CEO—who had the power to make things better but didn't. And when we did get concessions from them, it was most often too little, too late. The power to shape budgets and guide policy was what we needed, and that power lay elsewhere." Barack Obama (*A Promised Land,* 2020).

Notice how President Obama used the word *power.* While I am arguing that persuasion is more effective than power, I am not naïve to the fact that many liberal leaders want to dominate conservatives, and many conservatives will not consider that a liberal could raise valid concerns. Finding common ground is difficult because liberals can be irritating. Note Obama's reference to getting concessions. That is why the left is so annoying. They are constantly looking for concessions like the drip of a faucet. Although concessions are supposedly aimed at the rich, the problem from a conservative viewpoint is that they often affect all of us except leftist elites. It is not that conservatives are opposed to local job-training centers, after-school programs, and strengthening families; it is that we seek to find solutions that do not rely entirely on government.

One more quote from Obama tells us much about him and his wife Michelle:

> "Both of us were drained physically and emotionally, not only by the labors of the previous eight years but by the unexpected results of

an election in which someone diametrically opposed to everything we stood for had been chosen as my successor."

Trump is not the only politician to exaggerate, though he has been more proficient at it than most. I suggest that, when Obama says he and Trump are "diametrically opposed," Obama exaggerates. Trump appointed Ben Carson to implement Enterprise Zones that would help people in poorer inner cities. Obama had worked on revitalizing the same type of places. Both Trump and Obama claim to believe in "American Exceptionalism." Both Trump and Obama have said there is a goodness about America. Both wanted a better economy. Both embrace power politics. Both opposed the Iraqi War. Both ignored Russian involvement in Crimea. Both unmercifully criticized their presidential predecessors. (If it had occurred to Obama to rename San Andreas, he might have called it Bush's Fault.)

Certainly, there were and are numerous serious differences in the policies of President

Obama and President Trump, but they also have some things in common, and they would have more in common if they and their followers made such an effort. The idea that the left and right have nothing in common is not true.

The Value of Research

One thing that politicians commonly have available to them is research. For example, the findings of a strong relationship between the use of tobacco and the incidence of cancer. This research was the basis for regulation.

My Ph.D. research project was the most difficult venture I have ever undertaken. I understand why academics who have gone through the anguish of that experience become skeptics. As doctoral candidates go through the rigor of trying to do it right, it can become apparent that much research is not well done and, even when it is done rigorously, results can be inconclusive. My quantitative project conclusions were dependent on advanced statistics, which deal with probabilities. It may seem like a contradiction for me to hold that research adds to our *for-sure* knowledge while recognizing that it deals with probabilities. I will attempt a reconciliation.

The difference between probability and absolutes has to do with the sphere of knowledge being discussed. Probability generally has to do with predicting the future. A common example is weather forecasts. Meteorologists have formulas that include various factors like humidity, temperature, barometric pressure, and the movement of fronts. When they plug these and other variables into the formulas, they get a percentage of likelihood of rain, snow, or other weather conditions, in other words, a prediction. Certainty occurs in the present and recorded past. If it is pouring down rain on people, they are absolutely getting rained on at that moment. They may have noted the time of their soaking. However, it is not known for certain how long it will keep raining.

There are degrees of certainty as to how well we consider that our perception of reality truly matches reality. I have different amounts of expertise in various subjects. I have a minor amount of musical training. If asked to identify an eighth note, I would guess with a low degree of certainty. If I was asked to quote John 3:16 from the *King James Version of the Bible*, I could do this with a high degree of confidence that I had done so accurately.

If a person is to assert that there is no such thing as certain knowledge, he/she cannot know that with certainty. Certainty could exist outside of their experience. Of course, it is also true that someone may be certain that something is true when it is false. That sort of dilemma calls for discernment.

There was a time when the only knowledge I had was by observation and reason. When I was 14 years old, that changed. At that age, a disturbing thought came to me over the course of six sermons at a church where my folks had just started taking us. I heard the preacher repeatedly say that all of us had sinned. I had a friend who dismissed the idea with a cavalier attitude. I could not merely dismiss it. Either it was true or not true. Also, whether the preacher's statement about humanity's sinful nature was true or not true, I also had to consider the accompanying thought that Jesus had paid the penalty for my sin. I was not initially thrilled with the thoughts the preacher expounded from the Bible, but I did not reject those thoughts. Rather, I prayed to God that He would forgive my sin, come into my life, and I would try His way.

The Nature of Faith

God's way includes faith. Biblical faith is compared with sight. Both are ways to receive knowledge (Hebrews 11:1). Sight and the other senses: hearing, touch, taste, and smell, are ways of perceiving the physical world around us, whereas faith is the way to know spiritual truth. Faith comes by hearing (Romans 10:17), but it is not just picking up the sounds of a verse; it is the process of discerning thoughts. People can pick up sounds without perceiving thoughts (Isaiah 6:9). Faith comes by perceiving the Word of God (Romans 10:17) which often comes by preaching. Faith is a means for people to acquire knowledge.

Faith is a gift of God (Ephesians 2:8-9). Faith that leads to appropriate action produces a new life (James 2:17; John 3:16). Faith makes it possible for a person to walk with God (Hebrews 11). As people discern from Scripture that God is great beyond measure and His lovingkindness is delightful, they humbly submit to Him and value His presence, which leads to grace and peace.

The more important consideration regarding faith is its source rather than its amount. Like a small seed, faith can influence something large like a mountain. The issue is whether God puts it on a person's heart to do something very difficult. *Without* God it would be impossible. *With* God it is possible. As extensive as incivility is, God can use people to move it out of our discourse and eliminate it from our encounters.

When we experience something, there are several things going on at the same time. Our brain is processing information from our senses. We may have various thoughts of interpretation of what is happening. We may be experiencing emotions. Many regard a person's own experience as the most authoritative information possible.

We declare: "It was my experience, and you cannot criticize it."

I will not argue with this declaration. What we know best tends to be what our senses inform us of and the emotions we feel, but it could be helpful to challenge our interpretation of the experience. For many people it is not so much the hurt of a trauma that is disturbing as the misinterpretation of the event.

When Jesus heard that Lazarus was ill, it appears that He purposely delayed in going to see him. Lazarus died. Martha greeted Him with, "Lord, if you had been here, my brother would not have died" (John 11:21). Mary was questioning whether Jesus really cared about them. Jesus wept and others interpreted that to mean that He did care about them. Perhaps Jesus wept because He did not want to see His friends hurt. And yet, He let them hurt for a short time until He demonstrated his power over death by raising Lazarus from the grave. You may know all the details of the story, but if you conclude that Jesus does not care, you have made an error—an error that hurts beyond the loss of a loved one.

Our son Brian died when he was 16. The knowledge that Jesus conquered the grave is a great comfort to us. My wife Kristine and I believe that, in the next life, we will serve God together with Brian, and with our stillborn daughter Susan. As we subsequently encountered many people who had lost children, we discovered that most were not coping well because they thought God did not care. In contrast, my faith grew, and I believe even more strongly that Romans 8:28 is true. I believe that "all things work together for good to them that love God" because God would have to be incredibly great and caring to work such a tragedy as the loss of our children into something good.

That I receive some guidance by way of faith does not mean that I follow every thought that pops into my head. A great benefit to believing that there is such a thing as truth is the corollary that there is such a thing as error. It is possible for me to misinterpret what I take in by faith as well as what I take in through experience. Because I accept the possibility of error, I try hard to avoid it. I have tried to be careful in this book to make what I say match my understanding of reality.

I was diligent in following the protocols of scientific methodology in my leadership research. I will mix the results of that study with what I have learned through faith. I recognize they come through different means. However, they are much in agreement. As one of my seminary professors said, "Truth is truth, wherever you find it." In my experience, the same truth comes from different sources, a phenomenon which elevates my confidence that my thoughts match reality.

Chapter 4

The Political Spectrum

I believe there is such a thing as absolute truth through which we can understand, or become familiar with, a part of reality. Reality is huge, so we can only know a portion of it. Political policy is a realm of reality that can be expressed in continuums as well as binary (either/or) choices. A part of moral reality is making binary decisions, but that does not negate the existence of idealized continuums such as Aristotle's concept of seeking a "golden mean" between the extremes of deficiency and excess. Much of political reality can best be understood as finding, and acting upon, the best of a range of alternatives. Immigration, spending, and land use are examples where what is needed is a sweet spot that is not all-or-nothing, but rather a happy medium.

We should not try to eliminate immigration because the importation of highly motivated people stimulates our economy. But it is possible to be overwhelmed by more people than can be absorbed into the economy. Our immigration laws are a mess and that is one of the things I wanted to work on if I had been elected to Congress. Our laws need to allow a reasonable number to immigrate into America legally. Wealthy resort operators manage to get cheap labor while it is nearly impossible to legally work in seasonal agriculture. We must contend with the wealthy who benefit from cheap illegal labor to welcome conscientious hard-working people to assimilate into our country. We must also contend with the extreme progressive and liberal views of George Soros-type globalists whose efforts seek to cripple nations by destroying borders.

The commitment to serve and protect the Constitution is similar to the marriage commitment where there is fidelity to each other in sexual relations and yet compromise in such things as what we eat. There are times for fidelity to concepts such as to life, liberty and the pursuit of happiness. Then there are times for compromise regarding such issues as land use when deciding where to build a road. For example, the concept of freedom can be looked at as a continuum of different views with those on one side craving to do whatever they want, while those on the other side seek protection.

Left-Wing and Right-Wing

We use the terms left-wing and right-wing to describe political views. I think it is confusing to label both right-wing and left-wing extremists as totalitarian. It makes more sense to me to view right-wing extremists as anarchists and left-wing extremists as totalitarian. In general, leftists embrace more government as applied to debatable issues and right-wingers seek relatively less government in seeking solutions.

Anarchists do not want any government. While researching for this book, the only work I found on the internet specifically about civil government was by those claiming to be Christian anarchists. They evidently were not serious about applying Romans 13 where Paul says that civil officials are given their authority by God in order to punish wrong doers. Anarchists mistakenly think there are no benefits from government.

When I was in high school, I experienced a little anarchy. Farm equipment started disappearing from the fields of ranchers in Eastern El Paso County, Colorado. A dozen armed neighbors decided to do a stakeout in a field of ours where there were no houses. I had just taken one of the first National Rifle Association courses on gun safety. It was obvious some of the neighbors could have also benefited from the course as they put cartridges in the chamber and were not careful about where they pointed their firearms. In the moonlight, tensions rose as in the distance headlights began to approach us and then would go a different direction. At those moments I was more frightened by the loaded guns being waved about than I was by the possibility of approaching thieves.

Evidently, the thieves got wind of our stakeout, and the stealing stopped. Most of the ranchers recovered their equipment after a deputy sheriff found where the thieves had stockpiled the equipment south of Peyton. Law enforcement officers also discovered who the thieves were and brought them to justice. I much prefer well-trained law enforcement officers who represent a jurisdiction rather than vigilantes.

I devised a chart to help put differing political positions into perspective.

Left	Right
Totalitarian Socialist Liberal	Conservative Libertarian Anarchist
← More Government	Less Government →

On the right, one step back from anarchists are libertarians who want a minimal amount of government. John Locke, who inspired our founders, was a libertarian, as were some of the founders themselves, for example, Patrick Henry and Samuel Adams. The Articles of Confederation that were adopted as Americans gained their independence was a libertarian document. That confederation government was inadequate to secure the rights of Americans and so patriots held a convention which led to the writing of our present US Constitution.

One step back on the right from the libertarians are conservatives. I consider myself a conservative and I believe conservatives generally have many of the same core values as libertarians. However, we tend to have a much stronger practical nature. Our present constitution was written by conservatives. It is not a pure libertarian document offering absolute liberty. Our constitution contains compromises, yet it lays out a system that has secured more liberty for its citizens than any government since that of Moses. Incidentally, representations of Moses and the Ten Commandments have special places in Washington, D.C.

The slavery issue in this country illustrates a split between libertarians and conservatives. On one side, extreme libertarian Democrats valued their freedom to do whatever they wanted so much that they were willing to severely restrict the freedom of others by force. On the other side, abolitionist Republicans worked to extend an equal degree of freedom to all men. A similar contention exists today between Democrats who maintain that a woman has the right to terminate the life of her unborn child and Republicans who maintain that no human has the right to take the life of an innocent person.

Some mistakenly think conservatives are always hanging on to the past while left wing progressives are the innovators. That is false. Our founders were great innovators of government, and they were conservatives. They were not trying to hang on to the past. They were trying to obtain as much freedom as possible for themselves and for future generations. Conservatives continue to produce innovative solutions to political problems while those idealists on both sides of us produce little more than angst.

The Left and the Right and Christians

Political conservatism should enjoy the support of conservative Christians who have long enjoyed the benefits of living in the US. We are in danger of minimizing the contribution of those who shed their blood to guard our freedom, and at the same time trivializing the blood sacrifice of our Savior. Jesus did not die on the cross for us to go on living for ourselves only. When we take the Lordship of Jesus Christ seriously, we will submit all of our lives to Him, which includes our involvement in politics. I am not saying specifically what each Christian should do. I am saying that every Christian should seek what God would have their role be in the political world as well as in the church world. It is not politics that taints people. It is people who taint themselves by being disobedient to God.

On my scale, liberals are next to conservatives. However, they are on the other side of a divide between right and left. Liberals are mild leftists who generally would prefer to be described as moderates. The first half of the last century was marked by civil governance because it was largely a discussion between liberals with a Christian worldview and conservatives with a Christian worldview. Many liberals left the Christian anchor and drifted into becoming radical leftists who want to compel us to adopt progressive immorality. One hopeful development is a resurgence of liberals who do not go along with more radical leftists. Americans today are growing weary of leftist ideas that are more like a litany of *nag, nag, nag* than any semblance of creativity.

Socialism and Totalitarianism

The more radical thought, to the left of liberalism, is socialism. Socialists are on the left side of the spectrum. As such, they are counterparts to the libertarians on the right. Socialists are strong on ideology and short on practicality. Some of them may prefer to be called progressives, but from my perspective they are more digressive. Progressive/socialists have an overly optimistic view of mankind.

While it is unquestionably true that we have experienced remarkable scientific and technological advances, the moral advancement claimed by progressives is suspect. I agree that we have made progress in accepting people who are physically and culturally different, but we have also become more tolerant of increasingly gross sins.

In many countries, including the United States, welfare is a mild form of socialism. It is to help the neediest people to have basics necessary for survival. The Bible commends taking care of widows and orphans, as well as, making provisions for farmers to leave a portion of grain to be gathered by the poor in order that those in need would have enough to eat. Depending on the success of various welfare programs, especially in other countries, socialists claim those successes as their own in order to justify moving the United States further down the socialist road. An objection from people on the political right is that socialist programs can require an extensive expansion of government. Socialism can be more than a proposed remedy for income inequality. Full-blown socialism proposes the common ownership of resources which could theoretically be used to create wealth, but this is a myth because absolute socialism takes away the incentive to produce. Another objection, as voiced by former British Prime Minister Margaret Thatcher, is that, eventually, you run out of other people's money.

At the far left of the political spectrum are those who advocate for, and including those who operate, totalitarian governments. Totalitarian governments are counterparts of anarchists on the far right. Communism and Nazism are both on the far left. This is a much more appropriate designation than the unproductive labeling of right-wingers as Nazis. It is also more historically accurate. How much difference was there between the governance of Hitler and that of Stalin?

Outside the Political Spectrum

There is another category which exists outside the political spectrum I just described.

Some politicians and news media make political hay by labeling rebellious organizations as left-wing or right-wing and then glorifying or vilifying them. For such fringe groups, I prefer a label used by my dad for any disturber of the peace—knuckleheads. Whether labeled left-wing or right-wing, all individuals who violently attack legitimate institutions are knuckleheads who should be removed from the streets. It does not matter whether a disturber of the peace is wearing a white robe or a black robe, they should be fitted for orange prison jumpsuits and placed behind bars. Violent offenders who harm innocent people are the reason, as Paul described in his letter to the Romans, for public officials who are charged with keeping the peace. He wrote that governing authorities are God's servants to bear the sword to bring punishment on wrongdoers (Romans 13: 1-4).

A freedom-loving society must be especially diligent to protect peaceful protesters from harassment while also stopping anyone who attempts to loot or kill. Bullies should not be allowed to wear badges, and we need to understand that supporting violence to establish order by embracing Nazis or Communists is the surest way to have the worst rule established over us.

Good and Evil

Many are not aware of early Americans' Judeo-Christian view of justice. Therefore, there is a confusing mindset today whereby bad behavior is rewarded, and good behavior is punished. We are not the first nation to experience this dichotomy. The Old Testament prophets saw it as a terrible problem. Isaiah prophesied "woe to those who call evil good and good evil, who put darkness for light and light for darkness, who put bitter for sweet and sweet for bitter!" (5:20). Micah said it was the job of Israel's rulers to love the good and hate the evil and lamented that it was not that way (3:1-2). Malachi noted that his people did not see a problem with evil and they even declared that God was pleased with those who did evil (3:6).

People may not see a problem with rewarding evil and punishing good, but God does. Consider all which the Bible has to say on this subject:

> "The day of the Lord is near for all nations. As you have done, it will be done unto you; your deeds will return upon your own head," (Obadiah 13).

> "Tell the righteous it will be well with them, for they will enjoy the fruit of their deeds. Woe to the wicked! Disaster is upon them! They will be paid back for what their hands have done" (Isaiah 3:10-11).

> "For our offenses are many in your sight, and our sins testify against us. Our offenses are ever with us, and we acknowledge our iniquities: rebellion and treachery against the Lord, turning our

backs on our God, fomenting oppression and revolt, uttering lies our hearts have conceived. So, justice is driven back, and righteousness stands at a distance; truth has stumbled in the streets, honesty cannot enter. Truth is nowhere to be found, and whoever shuns evil becomes a prey. The Lord looked and was displeased that there was no justice," (Isaiah 59:12-15).

To restore civility, we must become humble before God so that we can follow His righteous commands. "Seek the Lord, all you humble of the land, you who do what He commands. Seek righteousness, seek humility" (Zephaniah 2:3). Some people think they are advocating justice when they are not. Others think it is impossible to be just. The fact that God requires justice means that justice is possible. The One who created us all is the One who gets to define justice. The Bible defines wickedness as disobeying God and righteousness as obeying God. "And you will again see the distinction between the righteous and the wicked, between those who serve God and those who do not" (Malachi 3:18).

What Does It Mean to Serve God?

Certainly, serving God means to obey the Ten Commandments plus Jesus' commands to love God and one another. In terms of governance, obeying God is also understanding and supporting conservative politics. Obeying God requires loving people (John 14). Love is more than a mushy feeling.

Serving God means helping people but trying to help people calls for wisdom. Reducing spending on programs like Medicaid can appear heartless. However, the responsibility for the budget-busting that Medicaid has caused is because of those who have tried to rely too heavily on government.

Love is seeking the best for others. Sometimes that means kindness and assistance. Sometimes love means letting someone suffer the consequences for their actions. When I was a commissioner, we established Drug Free

Delta County (DFDC). We worked with the county's drug court. Some in the program testified that getting arrested was the best thing that happened to them. Some jail time helped them get started on living a life of sobriety. The DFDC program relies heavily on volunteers. The budget of DFDC is minimal, especially compared to its benefits of restoring dignity, productivity, and turning societal takers into societal givers. DFDC is a heartfelt way to reduce the need for Medicaid. If this type of program was supported nationally, the cost of Medicaid would be dramatically reduced.

Conservatism should not be a callous rejection of assistance. Rather it is a coupling of assistance with a maintenance of dignity. Another great local program is facilitating people who are mentally challenged to live in small groups where they take care of themselves as much as possible. They go to work in the Salvation Army store where they fix things so they can be sold. Contributing to a community is good for the soul as well as for society. Feeling like we are making a difference adds important meaning to all of our lives and I believe it pleases God.

The DFDC and Salvation Army programs would not be possible without effective leadership. God is also pleased with those who offer the service of leadership.

Chapter 5

Leadership Matters

Mike Pence was one of the first to announce his candidacy for the 2024 Presidential election. My wife Kristine and I contributed to his campaign. Pence withdrew his candidacy before the first Republican debate. As I lamented over his fate, my first reaction was displeasure with some Christians who complain about the lack of morality on the part of politicians and yet would not lift a finger to help a moral candidate. Then, as I thought more about the situation, I remembered my doctoral research on the characteristics of effective leaders (Wolf, 2018).

In my research, one of the characteristics that I found to be highly correlated with accomplishment is a compelling vision. As I asked myself what vision Pence had communicated, I was unable to identify anything. Without a communicated vision, a leader will fade from the political scene. In contrast, candidate Donald Trump had established a very compelling vison. *Make America Great Again* touched the hearts of people who had increasingly endured anti-nationalist policies which diminished the power of the United States as a whole and demeaned its citizens individually.

My doctoral research has much to say about the relationship between accomplishment and certain leadership characteristics. Years of reading scholarly work about mentorship and transformational leadership preceded my doctoral research project, which was based on the career work of scholars Burns, Bass, and Leithwood, plus several research projects completed by others.

Burns (1978) was a historian with a particular interest in leaders who facilitated great change. He concluded that the key factor was what he called *transforming leadership*. In order to define transforming leadership, Burns began by contrasting it with *transactional leadership*, which is using rewards to motivate followers, such as offering political favors in exchange for support. While acknowledging that transactional leadership is powerful, Burns maintained that those who practiced transforming leadership were even more influential.

Based on the thoughts of Burns, Bass (1987) said that transformational leaders move beyond self-interest and contingent reward. Bass used the term *transformational* rather than *transforming* and then further described components of transformational leadership. I maintain that a transformational leader can also be described as a civil leader and, going forward, I will use those terms interchangeably. According to Bass, transformational leaders are inspirational, intellectually stimulating, good models and individually considerate. Based on my research, I modified Bass' concept of "inspirational" into the idea of <u>developing a mission vision</u>. And I modified his concept of intellectually stimulating into the idea of <u>encouraging careful thought</u>. In the long term, we need people with Mike Pence's morality and President Trump's vision.

Developing a Mission Vision Through Careful Thought

To develop an effective vision, a person must put much thought into what they want to accomplish in life. Figuring out who a person wants to be and what he or she wants to do is more important than paying consultants to come up with a catchy ad campaign. Ideally, a person should begin with the end in mind. Ask yourself: What do I want my eulogy to be? Anyone can be a better leader if they incorporate faith into their life plans.

Transformational leaders stimulate their followers to address problems and come up with solutions. Strategic planning is often needed to implement a person's aspirations. A transformational leader encourages others to think for themselves even if those thoughts differ from those of the leader. A transformational leader should also be a civil leader who can decipher the big picture, visualize small components and comprehend how the whole and the parts work together. Part of the reason that Dr. Martin Luther King was successful was because he understood American institutions and ideals. He gained the trust of his followers and expanded his leadership into successful strategies which were implemented in Montgomery and Selma. Careful thought leads to productive organization.

One example of Dr. King's behind-the-scenes organizational ability was his recruitment, in 1957, of James Lawson to join with Glenn Smiley a white minister from Texas as part of a two-man reconciliation team. They ran nonviolent workshops every Tuesday night throughout 1959 at the First Baptist Church of Nashville. They made Nashville a laboratory for demonstrating effective nonviolence (Hogan, 1997).

Bass (1998) said that transformational leaders can be counted on to do the right thing, showing high moral standards. They are consistent and persistent. They provide meaning to their followers' work. Followers will identify with leaders they admire, respect, and trust and they will want to emulate those leaders.

When we think things through, we can develop integrity. By faith, we can know that there is such a thing as truth—a truth which is more precious than gold. We must conform our lives to the Truth with a capital "T." We must be open to the removal from our lives of error in thought, word, and deed. Civil leaders are committed to consistency which is built on a strong foundation. Just as a skyscraper or bridge must be soundly anchored with a strong foundation and constructed out of pure materials, a strong life must be purposely directed and free of dross.

Being a Good Model

In my research project, the behavior most highly correlated with desired results was being a good role model (Wolf, 2018). In similar studies done by Estapa (2009) and Prater

(2004) modeling was also found to be the factor with the highest correlation for success. These results are consistent with Bandura's (2009) Social Cognitive Theory. Citing examples from the medical profession, Bandura pointed out that surgeons do not learn their profession by trial and error. They are careful to imitate a physician who has performed the surgery successfully hundreds of times. When I taught high school math, the quickest way to get students to solve a problem was to show them how to work through it on the white board. My adolescent learners could achieve even higher levels of reasoning in approaching complex problems when I showed them solutions step-by-step.

The power of example explains why incivility will not lead to civility. Preaching civility while practicing incivility will produce more incivility, including deviousness. There is truth in the old adage: "Your actions are so loud I can't hear what you're saying." The Old Testament provides numerous examples of how bad kings influenced the nation for evil and ruin while good leaders influenced people for good, which led to prosperity. As I pointed out in the first chapter, George Washington provided a great role model, especially of humility, and that model led to civility. He not only influenced his contemporaries; he helped form the enduring expectation on the part of American citizens that our leaders will be civil.

Accounting for Individual Differences

Civil leaders pay attention to each follower's need for achievement and such leaders act as mentors who nurture each follower's higher level of growth. The attuned leader shows an acceptance of individual differences and adapts methodology to the follower's needs and abilities. Civil leaders listen in order to develop whole persons, people who are not just seen as followers, but also as potential leaders. A civil leader helps others to grow into effective leaders themselves.

Civil leadership is exemplified by principle and self-sacrifice. It is said that if something is not worth dying for it is not worth living for. The martyred patriot Patrick Henry said, "Give me liberty or give me death." The signers of the Declaration of Independence believed in liberty and self-government so strongly that they were willing to pledge their property, reputations, and their very lives to make it happen. Subsequently, tens of thousands of Americans have made the ultimate sacrifice to protect our freedom.

Developing a mission vision, encouraging careful study, modeling desired behavior, and practicing individualized consideration are overlapping components of resonance, or in another word, *attunement*. I have borrowed the term attunement from counseling. It means to be able to relate to the thoughts, feelings, beliefs, needs, aspirations, and circumstances of others. Attunement is key to strong relationships and strong relationships are key to civil leadership. In order to return our country to more civil governance we need to be able to develop strong relationships with others.

President Abraham Lincoln and Dr. Martin Luther King Jr. are prime examples of resonance, being able to empathize deeply with people who have a similar cause. To a lesser extent, Senator Clinton, President Obama, and President Trump have resonated with people. When I was a Colorado representative to the National Association of Counties, I had an opportunity to hear Senator Clinton speak. She had done her homework and clearly spoke to our issues. In this instance, and on other occasions Hillary Clinton was better than Barack Obama at stirring up a crowd. Obama resonated with journalists. Journalists made President Obama into a rockstar. Donald Trump resonated with many who did not resonate with Clinton or Obama. Opposition does not necessarily diminish a person's leadership qualities. However, one's attitude toward opponents makes a difference. What distinguishes Lincoln, President Ronald Reagan and Dr. King from Clinton, Obama and Trump is an effort to relate to the opposition. A great leader sets goals to which everyone, even opponents, can aspire.

Lincoln promoted the ideal of sacrificing for a cause greater than self and combined that with an empathy for others. Lincoln and Stephen Douglas engaged in a series of spirited debates when the two men competed for election to the US Senate. In observing the debate in Quincy, Illinois in 1858, Carl Schurz noted that Lincoln had a "tone of earnest truthfulness, of elevated, noble sentiment, and of kindly sympathy which added greatly to the strength of his argument... Even when attacking his opponent with keen satire or invective something in his voice made his hearers feel that those thrusts came from a reluctant heart, and that he would much rather have treated his foe as friend" (Schurz, 1858).

Lincoln was a good conversationalist who also knew how to listen. He made sure his actions followed his words. He fueled his leadership with an unswerving commitment to something greater than himself (Leadership Lessons, 2020). Lincoln was attuned with the majority of Americans. Our most respected political leaders provide excellent examples of transformational leadership characteristics such as providing role models and paying attention to individuals while inspiring them to action that is productive within the American political system. Civil leadership is not unrealistic. It has been accomplished by leaders in the past and it can be accomplished again.

Details of My Research

Similar to the tobacco/cancer correlative studies, which are one of a dozen experimental and experiment-like studies (Campbell and Stanley, 1963), my correlative study focused on the correlation between the leadership characteristics of school principals and results on statewide standardized testing. The instrument that I used to determine the degree to which a principal had certain characteristics was a 34-item survey in which teachers rated their principal. The items for the four Bass characteristics were developed by Leithwood and Jantzi (1997) from whom I received permission for their use.

Each of the characteristics which I tested were represented by at least three items. Averages of each characteristic item were made so that the number of items would not affect the results. I analyzed the correlation of survey results of middle school principals' characteristics with results on a statewide standardized test: Colorado's Measure of Academic Success (CMAS).

Researchers often declare a level of probability to establish whether the results of a study are significant or not. A generally accepted level is $p=<.05$, which roughly means that the statistical probability of error is 5 percent or less. Out of nine characteristics I tested, five had $p=<.05$. Four of those statistically significant characteristics were based on items drawn from Bass's (1987) work on transformational leadership and were described earlier in this chapter. All four of Bass's transformational leadership characteristics had positive Pearson correlations of over 70 percent. (The Pearson correlation coefficient is an accepted standard for measuring the strength of association between variables.) For each of those four correlations to be that high it is likely that principals who had one of the characteristics also had others.

The point is that solid research supports the descriptions of effective leadership made in this book.

Survey Questions

Following are the survey items regarding four of the five characteristics most strongly correlated with higher standardized test results for Colorado eighth graders. I have included them here to help in understanding the meaning of the characteristics.

Characteristics Associated with Developing Aspirations through a Mission Vision:

- commanded respect from everyone on the faculty;
- excited faculty with visions of what we may be able to accomplish if we work together as a team;
- made faculty members feel and act like leaders; and
- gave the faculty a sense of overall purpose for its leadership role.

Characteristics of a Principal as a Role Model:
- led by "doing" rather than simply by "telling;"
- symbolized success within the profession of education; and
- provided good models for faculty to follow.

Characteristics of a Principal Who Practices Individualized Consideration:
- provided for extended training to develop my knowledge and skills relevant to being a member of the school faculty;
- personally helped me to develop my strengths;
- provided the necessary resources to support my implementation of the school program;
- treated me as an individual with unique needs and expertise; and
- took my opinion into consideration when initiating actions that affect my work.

Characteristics of a Principal Who Encourages Careful Thought:
- stimulated me to think about what I am doing for students;
- helped me to see the big picture;
- challenged me to reexamine some basic assumptions I have about my work in the school; and
- provided information that helps me think of ways to implement the school's program.

In this chapter, I have identified four leadership characteristics that are highly correlated with success. In the next chapter I will discuss three more leadership characteristics which are particularly successful in the context of educational policy. I started out researching transformational leadership. As I have stated earlier, since I have modified the concepts developed by Bass and added to them, I will continue to refer to my discoveries as civil leadership.

Chapter 6

Choice Choices for Big Ed

I like to think of public education as Big Education—or *Big Ed*. More than 90 percent of K-12 students attend public schools in America—some 48.1 million students (NCES, 2021). The Colorado legislature distributes over $7 billion to 178 local districts who are accountable to the state (Chalkbeat, 2022). Most counties in the state distribute more than half of their property tax revenue to school districts and more than half the state budget itself goes to K-12 education.

Private school educators have promoted various ideas to tap into that huge pot of money, but they are fighting an uphill battle to the extent that private schools are not accountable to the state. Without more funding, private schools are not likely to garner a larger share of students.

Charter schools are public schools that are subject to state regulation and oversight, albeit with waivers that allow them to cut costs. Handing out less funding per student while maintaining accountability is attractive to most fiscally responsible legislators. However, there is a limit to how much legislators are willing to rile teachers' organizations who do not want waivers that would lower their salaries.

I taught in a Christian school and in a charter school, as well as in regular public schools. I would be happy for private and charter school options to expand. However, even if private schools and charter schools were to experience unprecedented growth, Big Ed—in the form of regular public schools—will continue to educate the vast majority of K-12 students. The most productive thing that many conservatives can do for tens of millions of students is to get involved in regular public schools. Conservatives—and indeed all citizens—should show appreciation for teachers who are already taking the edge off the liberal deconstruction of our culture. Also, kudos to people like my dad who worked as a school board member to keep policies reasonable.

Encouraging Collaboration and Options

If students at all schools are our priority, then we should encourage collaboration. The Delta County School District fosters a generally cooperative relationship among education institutions. An example of what I thought was a great situation while I was at Vision Charter Academy was a student who took geometry from me, chemistry at the regular high school, music and language from a private school, and welding at the Technical College of the Rockies. As further evidence of cooperation, we devoted some geometry class time to figure out angles for her welding projects. And she planned to continue welding art projects after she graduated from high school.

Options are valuable commodities because we are all different. One of my doctoral study findings was that being aware of individual differences and adjusting expectations accordingly is a characteristic of principals whose students scored well on statewide standardized testing.

Examining Expectations

Some educators give emphasis to high expectations. One of the best-known research projects in the field of education was done by Rosenthal and Jacobson (1968) which they dubbed the Pygmalion factor. They compared two groups of elementary students. For one group, teachers were told that they were going to have an exceptionally good group of students the coming year. They called this the Pygmalion group. The teachers of a comparable control group of students received no instruction that would lead to higher expectations. Rosenthal and Jacobson reported that at the end of the year IQ tests showed that the Pygmalion group outperformed the control group.

In their criticism of the Pygmalion study, Flashoff and Snow (1970) noted that there was no expectancy advantage of students in grades three through six of the treatment group. Only students in the first and second grades showed an advantage from high expectations. One of the purposes of my research project was to identify factors for when high expectations are effective and when they are not. I found that, compared to high expectations alone, each Bass transformational leadership characteristic had higher correlations with academic achievement.

An important factor in achievement is whether or not the principal or teacher provides what is needed to be able to work toward those high expectations. In my study I found that students had the highest standardized test scores when their principals had high expectations and also delivered what was needed to meet those expectations. It is noteworthy that the principal whose students had the lowest test scores *was not* the principal who had the lowest expectations. Rather, that low distinction belonged to a principal who had high expectations but was the worst at delivering what was needed to meet those expectations.

As an example of delivering what was needed, one of my fondest teaching memories is when the principal got me the small tables that I wanted. I needed those more practical tables in order to quickly rearrange my classroom to fit the particular group or individual activities that went with my lesson.

In my teaching experience I found that reasonable expectations are important. One of the expectations which I think is reasonable is that all students will participate. At the beginning of the school year, I would point out that, to some degree, my students had chosen to be in my class and that I was paid to teach them math. There would be no discussion about what we were going to do in my class. We were going to work on math. Effective teachers are not content to forego students' class participation. An effective teacher will find out what a student is capable of and what they are interested in. An effective teacher will work with each student until each individual succeeds, knowing that the pattern of success will motivate individuals to achieve more success. I am dismayed that some teachers allow students to vegetate in their classes.

Toward a More Complete Definition of Civil Leadership

Based on my research findings, I added two characteristics to Bass's four in order to make a more complete definition of leadership. I added *reasonable expectations* and *management capabilities* to help meet those expectations. I then re-tested the survey items using those six characteristics in total. That combination produced a remarkable significance of less than .006 chance of error. The regression coefficient suggested that each additional unit of the six-characteristic leadership factor increased Colorado Measures of Academic Success scores by 13.7 (Wolf, 2018).

In my psychology and teacher preparation classes at Colorado State University, the emphasis was on Behaviorism. B.F. Skinner (1977) was a leader in that School of Psychology. He and others have done so much research verifying the concept of *contingent reward* that we can say it is a scientific fact. (In essence, contingent reward is a motivational approach to leadership which sets specific goals and objectives, then rewards people for achieving those goals and objectives.) My research and the work of others show that transformational leadership can be more effective than contingent reward. However, this in no way negates the truth that people can be influenced by making their behavior dependent on desired rewards. When applied to politics, I add that it is crucial for a system to reward productive behavior. However, when politicians offer rewards to individuals in exchange for support, the resulting behavior may have implications of bribery.

All of which inspired me to add a seventh characteristic which completes my definition of principles of effective leadership. That seventh characteristic is support for a system that rewards those who contribute to the public good. When I combine my reworking of Bass' four characteristics with the two characteristics discussed in this chapter, and add this seventh characteristic, that process yields a thorough definition of civil leadership. Here is my enhanced list of the effective characteristics of civil leadership:

1. Develops aspirations to accomplish a mission vision
2. Encourages careful thought and discussion to strategically carry out the vision
3. Humbly models the expected behavior
4. Accounts for individual differences
5. Expects respectful participation
6. Manages to supply followers with needed resources
7. Supports a system that rewards beneficial behavior

I suggest that these seven characteristics are the essential elements of civil leadership. My research has shown them to be effective.

If a behavior is not effective, it is not productive, and therefore it is not civil. Ineffectiveness leads to unrest. For the remainder of this chapter, I will discuss ineffectiveness as it relates to education.

The Decline of Academics

One of the problems with which educational leadership must deal is maintaining practical applications of academics. As a society we say science, technology, engineering and math (STEM) are of crucial importance. My experience is that we do not follow through. For example, since the academic conduct of my classes was continually interrupted by students going elsewhere to take part in non-academic endeavors, I often remarked that instead of *high school* it ought to be called *high activities.*

A reason that our young people do not do as well as other nations on standardized testing is because academics and test performance are not priorities of our society. Our culture is not conducive to standardized testing. Our accolades go to sports stars, not to academic stars. Many conservatives think education is the province of states and local districts. However, one mission the US Department of Education could take on is encouraging students to do well on standardized testing by having contests with well-publicized results. More local school leagues could have academic days where students compete. In Colorado we have structures in place to have state championships in sports, band, debate and spelling. We need to add history, math and other subjects. If we think practical academics are valuable, we will find more ways to reward academic achievement.

Another reason for poor academic achievement is a lack of a high purpose. A colleague complained that the Christian schools took all the good students and that is why they did better on testing. My observation was that the Christian school students were in many ways similar to public school students. However, the reason they did better was because they had a sense of higher purpose and did not have cold water thrown on them in an effort to quench that essential fire.

The Erosion of Respect for Authority

Another difference is that Christian school parents tend to instill a respect for authority. One day, while I was substituting for a teacher at a public middle school, I heard a *tink-tink-tink* sound coming from a desk to my right. I pretended to look toward the sound, but I was focused on the back of the room, in search of the source. Out of the corner of my eye, I saw Chip Block (not his real name) throwing broken pieces of colored pencils across the room.

I wrote up a behavior slip and sent Chip to the office. Afterward, the principal informed me that students had been told that if they got a behavior slip that day, they would not be able to go to the dance that night. Chip's dad called to complain about the punishment. The principal told the father that it would be up to me whether or not I should withdraw the behavior slip. I said no, it should stand.

Mr. Block called me at home after school to give me an earful, chiding me for being so unfair to Chip by writing him up for such a harmless thing when so many students were doing worse things. I said there was not much misbehaving going on in the school and that Chip's actions were not so minor. Chip had destroyed school property, and he could have struck someone in the eye. My underlying concern was a lack of respect. I didn't have many rules in the classroom: Respect me; respect each other; and respect school property. In the greater educational world, respect would go a long way toward establishing civility.

There were plenty of times when I was merciful to students, but I attached mercy to repentance. Chip and Mr. Block were not sorry. There was no indication that they would make an effort to see that it did not happen again. As a society, we seem to be getting worse in not respecting authority. This lack of respect has led to incivility.

In the high plains community where I grew up, parents and teachers were pretty much on the same page. That united front meant there was a lot of schoolwork and not much horsing around in the school setting.

In my Chip Block situation, parents of that bygone era would not have advocated for their child to go to the dance. Instead, they would have grounded their son from other activities as well.

Behind the respect and cooperation which prevailed in my youth was a unity of purpose. My mom was president of the Parent-Teacher Association until that group's liberal bent inspired her to become president of the more independent Parent Teachers' Organization. So, she was the last president of the local PTA and the first president of the local PTO. I overheard a mild complaint from her that they couldn't meet on Wednesday evenings because the elementary school teachers had prayer meetings then. The school's annual Christmas program was the biggest event of the year, and its content was evidence of an evangelical influence. Before the bags of candy were handed out to families, the community voluntarily and robustly sang:

"He rules the world with truth and grace and makes the nations prove the glories of His righteousness and wonders of His love." Those thoughts exude purpose.

The Element of Chance

Consider the following two statements:
1. Everything came into existence through natural chance occurrences.
2. Everything came into existence through the purposeful acts of a being outside of nature.

Neither statement is, in itself, more logical than the other. Neither statement is more scientifically verifiable than the other. Neither statement is an establishment of religion, unless students are denied an opportunity to freely express both statements.

I think natural selection is a scientific fact. There is evidence that some life forms came into existence over an extended period. I have no problem with evolution being taught encompassing those two concepts.

However, the more over-reaching concept that all life came into existence through one chance development after another is a fallacy which I call "evil-lution." We should use reason and political influence to see that evil-lution is not a part of state curriculum standards. All students should have a reasonable opportunity to choose a personal purpose, unhindered by public schools. When it is recognized that another person has purpose, then it follows that we will respect them and lovingly seek to help them find and carry out their purpose.

The emphasis of evil-lution in the classroom discourages students from believing there is a Creator who loves them and has a purpose for their lives. I have been respectful of school district policies to not teach religion in the classroom. As a result, I have emphasized an important second-best approach which manifests itself in the following examples.

Encouraging Sparks

As a high school homeroom teacher, I encouraged students to discover their sparks of interest that could flame a productive career. As an Academic Manager for Job Corps, I was pleased to continue helping students prepare for productive vocations.

The Reformation called attention to the concept of a calling. A person's vocation was viewed as a calling from God. This resulted in a respect for work that led Europe out of the Dark Ages and into prosperity. A restoration of the concept of vocational accountability to God could help lift us out of our current cultural recession. A respect for trade education and careers would also help.

Jesus provides the greatest example of civil leadership, including developing aspirations such as following one's calling. Scientifically conducted research has shown that principals who have civil leadership characteristics have students who perform better on standardized tests. To improve all our schools, we should choose to encourage principals to be more like Jesus.

Chapter 7

A Calm Assessment of Socialism

We came very close to electing a self-proclaimed socialist to the presidency in 2020. If several Democratic candidates had not withdrawn from the race in favor of Joe Biden, or if Elizabeth Warren had dropped out, Bernie Sanders would have become the Democratic candidate and then likely have been elected to occupy the White House.

This was not an overnight development. People in academia have been advocating for a fair distribution of wealth for decades. Liberal college professors influenced teachers who influenced youth to the point that a majority of young people now view socialism as a good thing in contrast to capitalism which is portrayed as an inherently unjust system that encourages the exploitation of poor people and the environment. Older Americans prefer capitalism to socialism 68 percent to 32 percent (Gallup, 2019). Sanders has led a vigorous charge against income inequality while advocating a governmental redistribution of wealth as the solution. There is a dark side to socialism that was exemplified by the Union of Soviet *Socialist* Republics. I will touch on this later, but for now I would like to address income redistribution.

In 1970, I took a course at Colorado State University on the Economics of Poverty. The professor presented the idea of a negative income tax, where workers below a poverty line would receive money via the IRS. The negative income tax took the form of the Earned Income Credit which was signed into law by President Nixon.

A few years later, my wife and I qualified for the Earned Income Credit. We filled out a 1040 Income Tax form. Instead of having to pay income tax, the Internal Revenue Service sent us a check for about $1,000, which we promptly put into the local economy. Neither the nationally known politicians advocating socialism, nor those opposing socialism have discussed the merits, or lack thereof, of increasing the Earned Income Credit. Perhaps this is because these individuals have never had a job working long hours for low pay.

COVID and Civil Measures

Though President Trump vowed the United States would never be a socialist country, he proposed, and Congress approved, two payments to people during the COVID pandemic. The stated goal was to stimulate an economy that had been substantially shut down by regulations which purported to slow the spread of the virus. Republicans and Democrats passed legislation to send all Americans a check for $1,200, even if they had not been working. That was socialism in the sense of a redistribution of wealth.

However, general agreement on the stimulus checks is an example of civil governance in the midst of heated rhetoric by socialists about the evils of capitalism and by libertarians on the evils of socialism. President Trump and many Democrats wanted another distribution of $2,000. Senate Majority Leader Mitch McConnell called that proposal socialism for the rich. The Senate and House reached a compromise of $600 per person. By popular definition, these actions were civil because they were preceded by reasoned discussions.

Roots of Inflation

To pay for some of their spending, the federal government prints more money. That is the root of most American inflation. We all pay for these transactions in the form of higher prices for commodities. If these somewhat higher prices are the only debt we are paying for, it might be worth it to keep a stable economy. Delta County avoided debt. The county could not print more money. Thankfully, most of our government is local. If our government were predominately national, we would be in much worse financial shape than we are.

One reason for those COVID-era share-the-wealth distributions was that they would stimulate the economy. When I served on the Colorado Board of Human Services, I justified my conservative presence there as a way to help small businesses. What do small businesses need most? They need customers. Most of Human Services' clients were not savers. They spent their assistance, often at small businesses. So, this modest application of sharing-the-wealth socialism can contribute to the raising of income levels beyond those who are direct recipients.

During the terms of Colorado Governor Bill Owens (2001-2009), Republicans did not cut programs designed to help needy people. Republicans did work hard to make those programs efficient and sought innovative ways to fund the programs so that the cost to taxpayers was minimized. In the United States we have a mixed economy of wealth-producing free enterprise which also regards the welfare of all through government and non-profit (including churches) sharing the wealth.

A Little Socialism

Dad often said, "A little socialism is a good thing." My family shares some ownership and revenue. Sharing wealth has been a good thing for us. Corporations are share-the-wealth organizations and, as such, are socialist, although they can be used to raise capital, making them both socialist and capitalist. Socialism can work at the tribal level. The Southern Utes divide their revenue from natural gas amongst themselves. The tribe supports a Boys and Girls Club in Ignacio—something which I wish we had in Delta, Colorado.

During my college anthropology course, I learned that Margaret Mead considered socialism to be an offshoot of Christianity. The book of Acts describes the early church as holding things in common, perhaps as an extension of Jesus and the Twelve who appeared to have a common purse. However, both were temporary devices to facilitate intensive teaching. They were voluntary—not operated by a government. As soon as believers numbered in the several thousands, they abandoned common ownership, although enclaves remain in communes and monasteries even today.

Despite what Garth Brooks sang, too much of a good thing *is not* a good thing. The fire that warms can become the fire that burns. Helping people is heart-warming. Co-dependence can be destructive. I am concerned that a sizeable number of Americans have come to prefer getting handouts from the government rather than working. Like drug addicts, their appetites can become insatiable. In the United States we must strive to adequately meet needs while avoiding co-dependency. Funding programs just for the sake of getting votes is not civil, even if you can quietly get Congressional leadership support.

TANF and Medicaid

When $283 billion from the states is added to the federal contribution, some $1.03 trillion was spent on 80+ welfare programs

(Budget, 2022). Two of the major US welfare programs are Temporary Assistance to Needy Families (TANF) and Medicaid.

TANF was a compromise program by the Clinton administration and the Newt Gingrich led Congress to replace the Aid to Families with Dependent Children (AFDC) program. Over time, AFDC was costing more and was inadvertently encouraging single-parent families. TANF funding was capped in 1996, and part of the program now is to encourage two-parent families. Recipients are not going to get rich on the few hundred dollars a month from TANF they get for a maximum of 60 months. However, in combination with other welfare programs, recipients may live adequately and receive training to qualify for jobs. TANF is beneficial because it encourages people to work.

Medicaid is a federal and state program that helps with medical costs for people with limited income and resources. It is difficult for Colorado and other state legislatures to come up with enough funding for Medicaid. Currently in Colorado, that funding is not enough to cover the costs of Medicaid patients to physicians and hospitals.

When I looked into Medicaid, it appeared to be flawed so that it rewarded bad behavior. A person may be struggling with drug addiction and not find help, but if he completely ruins his health he can get on Medicaid. A Medicaid patient who has overdosed can demand to get into an emergency room, wreak havoc, and gain admittance until he feels better. Then he can refuse treatment that would help him stay sober, only to return to the emergency room the next time he overdoses.

Not all bad behavior is on the part of patients. New York Governor Andrew Cuomo's administration was found to be careless in putting COVID patients in the same nursing home facilities as frail elderly. As of January 14, 2021, it was reported that 38 percent of all COVID-19 deaths were residents of nursing homes (Ochieng, 2021). COVID highlighted a problem of deficiencies in long-term health care institutions (Werner, 2020). Evidently, the warehousing of the elderly, whose hearts were kept beating beyond the normal function of other organs, quickly took its toll. The huge cost to taxpayers might lead a person to think that the majority of the elderly are in nursing homes. Not so. Eighty to ninety percent of long-term care is done outside of nursing homes. I appreciate home health care and am pleased that we were able to provide for our mom and dad at home during their last years. It was a burden for us four kids, so I appreciate how difficult it is for one or two siblings. The Apostle Paul said that whoever would not help his family was worse than a heathen, but some don't have families and there can be illnesses that require special care, so there is a place for nursing homes

When the Old Testament prophet envisioned the Messianic Kingdom, he said people will build houses and dwell in them. They will plant vineyards and eat the fruit. No longer will they build houses and others live in them, or plant and others eat (Isaiah 65:21-22). The structure of a prosperous nation is such that people can predict if their work will be rewarded. The principle is the same in the New

Testament. The Apostle Paul warned believers that "If a man will not work, he shall not eat" (2 Thessalonians 3:10). The Plymouth colonists nearly starved as they began with a socialist system but prospered as they adopted the work-to-eat rule endorsed by Paul.

A Tipping Point

One of the tipping points where socialism becomes destructive occurs when it takes away an individual's incentive to produce. Isaiah and Paul both said that people should receive the fruit of their labor. Extensive research has demonstrated the same point. B.F. Skinner and other Behaviorist psychologists taught operant conditioning (stimulus-response) as the key to understanding human behavior. In layman's terms it is rewarding the desired behavior. According to Skinner, if the controller is not getting the desired response, it is because he is using the wrong stimulus. Stimulus-response works to bring prosperity to Americans as evidenced by our development of natural resources which has generated wealth. While exploitation at the expense of others, and waste, should be condemned, producers who work hard for the benefit of all of us must be rewarded.

Socialism is a tough sell unless people accept the lie that you can have everything you want for free. Socialist tyrant Joseph Stalin took away peoples' freedom and gave them crumbs. The Union of Soviet Socialist Republics was notorious for shortages because there was a lack of incentive for anyone to produce needed commodities until Stalin manufactured special artificial incentives. Was it fair for him to single out certain people for incentives?

Leftists are not reasonable when they propose to reward idleness and deny rewards for productive behavior then call these actions a crusade for justice. A co-worker told me that his daughter refused to go to work because she could make more through various welfare programs. The United States cannot afford for many to reach that conclusion. There is much to be said for the idea that people who choose security over freedom deserve neither security nor freedom.

Chapter 8

Abortion and the Use of Law for Social Change

It is said, "You cannot legislate morality." It may be true that we cannot make people moral by passing a law, but it is also true that laws should be moral. When discussing any public policy, the first question should be "What is right?" Only when we ask this question can we evaluate the best way to encourage the right behavior. It is impossible to legislate and enforce every moral issue. We must be strategic in using the power of government.

Jesus said, "Blessed are those who hunger and thirst after righteousness for they shall be satisfied." An individual's hunger and thirst for righteousness can begin in this life, but the ultimate satisfaction will not come until all are under the complete rule of God.

In the past, this nation has been blessed when a majority of people sought righteousness. At present, our nation is suffering under the burden of so many who hunger and thirst—not for righteousness—but rather to satisfy the fantastic desires of their bodies without regard for the actual needs of others or for the wonderful love of our Creator. The dilemma for Americans who want right and moral legislation in our nation is how to maintain the overall value of having a government of the people when a majority of people are wrong about a fundamental moral truth.

In resolving this dilemma, our mission becomes, first of all, one of persuasion, and second of all, persuasion, and third, persuasion. Having convinced people, we must seek legislation, followed by continual persuasion to maintain moral thoughts and practice. I will begin with some arguments for a moral position on abortion and then move to practical possibilities for moral legislation.

The Persuasion Mission

A problem in trying to resolve the abortion issue is the effective deceptiveness of many pro-abortion advocates. Perhaps the most consequential idea regarding abortion is that it is of no consequence. The disposal of non-descript tissue is viewed by some as no big deal (except when it becomes a commodity to sell). The less human the unborn is thought to be, the easier it is to get rid of it. The Nazis' Final Solution portrayed Jews as vermin that should be exterminated. To counter such narrow thinking, the most effective tools of pro-lifers are photos and videos which show how human the unborn are.

During the first decades of my life, I participated in our family ranch operation. Each year most of our 300 cows had calves. During calving season, we took turns checking the first-calf heifers every three hours. If there were difficulties, others in the family were called out to assist. In helping so many cows for some 30 years, we never encountered a situation where we felt the need to kill the calf in order to save the cow. Is human biology so inferior to bovine biology that millions of abortions must be performed in order to save the lives of human mothers? Can some difficult situations be taken care of with compassionate good judgement or are we doomed to have abortion free-for-alls in many states?

Perhaps the difference in numbers for humans and for cows is more a matter of economics than of physiology. Whereas it is in the ranchers' financial interest to aid life, it is more lucrative for the abortion mill operators to purvey death.

For the abortionist it can be a matter of money. For many who cooperate with the procedure the benefit is convenience. It enables men and women to enjoy the pleasure of sex without accepting the responsibility of raising a child. The sexual revolution of doing whatever you feel whenever you feel like it has resulted in the revolting development of cheapening our view of life. Every life matters whether it is an athlete like Tim Tebow or a kid with Down's Syndrome.

God values us. He put us here to be able to make a decision of whether we want to have an abundant life or not. Short-circuiting that plan has huge consequences.

Abortion practice is insidious. It is not just aborting the pregnancy early. It is about killing the baby even when it could survive outside the womb. Adoption is a non-murderous option.

It seems like it should be easy to convince people who are not totally hedonistic that abortion is wrong. The tough part is figuring out how to stop hedonistic people from killing their babies.

A Lincoln Day Challenge

In my first Lincoln Day Dinner as a county commissioner candidate, a stalwart Republican challenged me on my public pro-life stance. I hope those who criticize pro-life candidates for not ending abortion will see that it is not as easy as it may appear. Part of the difficulty is the large number of Republicans who want us to stay out of the fray because they see abortion as a distraction from a greater mission which they think is to limit government in all matters. Some church people also think the abortion issue is a distraction from evangelism.

In 2005, there were 11,622 abortions in Colorado. In 2015 there were 8,333. That decrease coincides with my observation of pro-life people keeping the issue before the people by signing petitions, supporting pro-life candidates, and proposing legislation. From 2015, abortions in Colorado steadily increased through 2022 when there were 14,154. This increase coincides with my observation that libertarians have increased their resistance to the pro-life movement.

A factor in this trend is my right-wing libertarian brothers' acceptance of the notion that the reversal of Roe v. Wade will lead to government prosecution. This is truly not inevitable.

From 1930 until the Roe v. Wade ruling, there was not one woman who was prosecuted for having an abortion. We must return to that position as a practical matter. There have recently been some sensationalized reports on social media of women being prosecuted for having a miscarriage. We do not need to check out whether the miscarriage was natural or induced. If we do not consider the libertarian concerns in this matter, we are going to see increasing resistance to our efforts and we will see fair weather pro-life politicians running for cover. We need to be sensitive to the few mothers who need special delivery care.

Public policy can change, and it can change back, depending on the motivation of people towards various causes, including pro-life. The Republican party was not pro-life in the 1970s. It took pro-lifers getting involved in party politics to change that. If we give up, it can change back. Democratic President Jimmy Carter was pro-life. Subsequently, people took over the Democratic Party who think special civil rights should be extended to sexual deviants and for women to have a right to abortions.

If enough right-thinking people participated in the Democratic Party, their influence could make it possible for a pro-life candidate to be nominated. Would it not be great to have a choice of two pro-life candidates like we did with Presidents Carter and Reagan?

What Kind of Laws?

If we had civil and pro-life leadership, what kind of laws would it be wise to have?

David the king said that he loved the law. Paul the missionary emphasized that the law could not save anyone. In the evangelical churches where I have experienced fellowship, we spent much more time in Galatians than in the Psalms. In our zeal to emphasize the important point that salvation is by grace and not by works we have neglected the important use of the law in guiding a society.

Just as building roads is a proper function of government, so is building a social structure that facilitates productive behavior and discourages destructive behavior. We could complain that public roads do not allow us to drive our cars everywhere. We could also complain that laws restrict us from doing anything and everything that occurs to us. Guardrails on dangerous sections of public highways are there for our protection. So are legal guardrails.

The time when the Republican party was the bastion of law and order has passed, and we need to get back to it. The time when the Democratic party observed laws that protected people is a distant memory which should again become reality. My experience in county government was that liberals promoted regulation while libertarians were vocal in their opposition. However, once a regulation was adopted, I found that some liberals ignored the law by acting as if it only pertained to others while most libertarians I knew were careful to follow the letter of the law, even when they did not agree with it.

A nation needs laws to make it whole and civilized. Individuals need the presence of the Holy Spirit to be whole. While Galatians 2:8-9 declares that we are saved by grace through faith that is a gift of God, Galatians 2:10 adds that we are His workmanship created to do good works. We should not get the cart before the horse, but we should also not disregard the cart. When a person is born of the Spirit, God gives us the ability to follow the law. John 1 says that children of God will not make a practice of sin. When we acknowledge our sin, God forgives us and cleanses us. Believers are not only delivered from the penalty of sin but also from the power of sin.

A History of Conservative Activism

In general, conservatives support less government, but conservatism is not just about quantity of government. It is also about *governmental quality*—about the best way to protect life, liberty and the pursuit of happiness. For most of America's history it was conservatives who initiated change through government. Conservative pastors fomented the American Revolution. Conservatives drafted our constitution because they were more concerned than libertarians about securing liberty to protect the rights of everyone. Christian Republicans led the call for the abolition of slavery against libertarians who wanted to hang on to their liberty at the expense of the liberty of those they chose to demean. Through the suffrage movement, religious women won the right to vote.

Conservative religious Christians also fueled the campaign against drunkenness that ensnared families. As the industrial revolution gained steam, some men got in the habit of dropping by the local tavern on their way home from work, wasting money that should have gone to provisions for their family. Many drunkards were also unpleasant to deal with in that condition.

People in general, and women in particular, got fed up with the social problem of drunkenness. Concerned citizens began pushing for legislation to close taverns. It would have been interesting to see if such a limited regulation would have been effective. But as often happens in populist causes, the more radical leaders gained control of the temperance movement and pushed for a total ban on beverages containing alcohol. The 18th Constitutional amendment began prohibition on January 17, 1920.

I am one who believes drunkenness is always wrong. I also believe that legislating against drunkenness is not off limits just because it is a moral issue. However, I think we can learn some things from the legislative attempts to deal with drunkenness.

Prohibiting a family from having a glass of wine over dinner is tyranny. Most Americans went along with the ban anyway, but a significant number did not. Bootlegging of hard liquor became rampant. Trying to stop even the most flagrant offenders proved difficult. Organized criminals who were raking in the money were able to influence some police officers. Corruption plagued enforcement against large-scale offenders. Bootlegged liquor made Al Capone and his cronies wealthy.

Eventually, Americans realized that prohibition was causing more social ills than it was preventing. They voted for the 21st Amendment which ended the prohibition of alcoholic beverages on December 5, 1933—just 13 years after it began. The temperance movement showed that even people with a generally conservative outlook can get caught up in pushing for excessive government, especially those who are more religious than relationship oriented. The challenge for leaders who seek to change the law in order to change society is to keep the aspirations of their followers realistic.

After the embarrassment of prohibition, many Evangelicals retreated from social causes, especially those involving government. Liberals were eager to fill the void. Much of today's liberal agenda has to do with sexual ethics. There might be some credence to the position of the religious-minded abstaining from some moral issues. However, this position is only credible if people with a secular viewpoint would also stay out of such issues but that is not the case. Secularists have gained power to legalize their hedonistic sexual morals.

Judicial Over-reach

In 1973, liberal Supreme Court justices exceeded their duties in codifying the legality of human induced abortion of unborn babies. The purported reason was to stop forcing poor women into back alleys to undergo coat-hanger procedures. The real reason was to protect medical doctors from being charged with murder for killing humans. Roe vs. Wade was about protecting enterprising physicians and not about protecting women, especially the female victims of abortions. There is no God-given right to an abortion. Regulations established by humans can be changed.

As a whole we have become what the Bible warns against: calling evil good and good evil. It is difficult for me to understand why people who purport to stand up for the underprivileged do not want to support the most underprivileged of all. It only takes the slightest imagination to realize the bloodiness of an abortion. How can anyone be so dull to think that cutting up a baby is right?

It was a leftist Supreme Court that tried to create a right for physicians to take the lives of unborn children. It was a leftist New York state legislature that cheered the establishment of legal protection for killing humans up to and including natural birth. Hearing the report of the celebration by the majority of the legislature and by Governor Cuomo reminded me of the Roman colosseum where crowds roared with approval as lions ripped innocent people apart. And they loved to have the choice of thumbs up or thumbs down on whether or not a victorious gladiator should slay his potential victim. Christians took over the governance of Rome from pagans and ended lethal spectacles. Will pagans continue to take governance of America away from Christians?

The recent Supreme Court decision to dismantle Roe v. Wade is a promising development but we must remain vigilant as the controversy has now been delegated to individual states.

As a Coloradoan, it is disgusting and embarrassing to me that our state legislature has tried to outdo New York's earlier celebration. Our slogan could now be "Come to Colorado. Get high and kill your baby at the same time." Colorado is going downhill with a liberal legislature and State Supreme Court. Florida offers some hope for Colorado. Florida had become a Mecca for people to have abortions who could not get them in their nearby state. Limiting abortions in Florida has had a huge impact in reducing abortions in the Southeast. Limiting abortions in Colorado could have a great impact on the Rocky Mountain region.

The Contraception Distraction

One of the distractions from limiting abortions is the muddying by both sides on the issue of contraception. Contraception and abortion are distinctly different, and they must be understood that way in order to get legislation passed. Most Americans think contraception is a noble practice and it is counter-productive to try to limit it at a legislative hearing. Abortionists know this and some of them try to sell abortion as contraception.

Dr. Larry Dillon is a strong pro-life advocate who supported me in my candidacy for county commissioner. Doc explained to me that many fertilized eggs pass through a woman's system without attaching to the uterus. Without implantation there is no pregnancy. And until there is a pregnancy there is no possibility of abortion. There are several ways to prevent pregnancy.

If a woman is raped or otherwise has unplanned sexual intercourse, she can take a morning after pill that will prevent a pregnancy. The morning after pill contains levonorgestrel which is a synthetic form of the hormone progestin. Levonorgestrel will prevent a pregnancy if taken within 72-120 hours of sex, but it will not harm an established pregnancy (Mayo Clinic, 2020). The estimated time that it takes for the sperm to travel to the egg and fertilize it is around six days after intercourse. Once it becomes fertilized, the egg can attach itself to the uterine wall.

While levonorgestrel will not harm a pregnancy, RU-486 contains mifepristone which ends a pregnancy and is most often taken with misoprostol to help expel the dead baby. The combination of mifepristone and misoprostol often costs more than $300 and requires a prescription plus physician monitoring, while levonorgestrel can be purchased over the counter without restriction at a local pharmacy for $30. The argument that the purpose of legalized abortion is to help poor women is bogus and deceitful. Abortions can cost ten times as much as a morning-after pill and often cost much more than that ten-fold amount. Do abortion doctors perform their "services" free of charge? According to the website comparably.com (2022) the average income of an abortion "doctor" in Denver is $117,546 per year. That is enough to make some substantial contributions to campaigns to expand abortion through legislation. Christians have not been matching abortionists' political spending.

A Line of Demarcation

Pope Alexander VI established a line of demarcation that became the basis for dividing the colonial interests between Spain and

Portugal. That is why Brazilians speak Portuguese, and the rest of Latin America speaks Spanish. We must establish a line of demarcation on the abortion issue at the point where a fertilized egg implants on the uterine wall. Before that moment the pro-choice language is appropriate. Women should have a choice about whether to get pregnant or not. Many options are readily available to prevent a pregnancy. That includes abstinence from sexual relations, which is 100 percent effective in reducing the possibility of pregnancy. Almost all of the attempted justifications for abortion can be taken care of by preventing a pregnancy which then makes an abortion unnecessary. American legislatures have not prevented a person from having access to numerous methods of preventing pregnancies.

The line of demarcation is a matter of governance. The various methods of contraception are subject to ethical debate and persuasion. Those ethical debates can help a morally sensitive person discern God's will in regard to having a spouse and children in their lives. However, debating contraception in a state legislature is less productive. Today's American legislators are not going to prohibit contraception. Including contraception in any legislation or citizen's initiative is like tying it to an unnecessary anchor—a practice which will assure that the legislation or initiative will sink. Including contraception will ensure that pro-choice language will influence peoples' opinions.

As soon as a fertilized egg attaches to a uterus, pregnancy begins and the pro-life language becomes appropriate. Pro-lifers have been willing to make legislative accommodations for rare cases. But rare cases do not justify the free-for-all slaughter of innocent Americans. Even where there might be a justification for an abortion, that does not automatically include a right to kill the aborted baby. If an aborted baby can live with medical assistance, then that medical assistance must be provided and the baby adopted as soon as possible.

Return to Persuasion

The success of the pro-death and anti-abortion movements should not be measured exclusively by legislation. The main tool of conservatives has always been persuasion. To the extent that we can help instill a pro-life sentiment in the hearts of some who would otherwise have an abortion, we have succeeded. Prohibition did not end drunkenness. The revocation of Roe vs. Wade will not keep some women from having abortions. Our work is not primarily done through legislation. We must continue with friendly persuasion and assistance.

We need to be respectful and truthful. Nevertheless, we need to remain mindful that the issue has gore at its core. I appreciate efforts to show people what abortion is. If it is too bloody to watch, then it is too bloody to practice. We must counter pro-death rhetoric that tries to include abortion under an umbrella of birth control. Birth control is commonly thought of as preventing pregnancy. *There is an enormous, and undeniable, difference between preventing a pregnancy and ending a pregnancy*. We should persuade fellow pro-lifers that the threat of prohibiting birth control unwittingly fuels the pro-choice/pro-death movement.

Conservatives have been working for decades to undo the damage done by liberals from 1955-1975, while liberals have doubled down on issues like abortion. For some time, the Hyde Amendment served as a compromise where Congress would not fund abortions while otherwise letting Roe vs. Wade stand. Nevertheless, President Obama broke that agreement in using federal funding for abortions.

I will continue to argue that early term abortion is immoral but enforcing laws against it are viewed by many swing voters as too much governmental interference. We who oppose abortion need to strive to achieve as much restriction of abortion as we can realistically implement. Perhaps, as the public sees that abortion opponents can be reasonable and compassionate in our enforcement of some restrictions, they will accept more. Contemplating early abortions is a sober matter. New life is a cause for celebration. Terminating that life is horribly sad. Harassing pregnant women, whether legal or not, is not an antidote for relieving that despair.

Immorality Versus Illegality

Getting drunk in a person's own home is immoral, but I do not want to make it illegal. That does not mean I sanction drunkenness. To try to regulate the amounts of beverages a person consumes in their home would be tyranny.

Speaking against God is immoral, but I do not want to make it illegal. That does not mean I condone blasphemy. Trying to regulate blasphemy could become tyrannical.

To desire what belongs to another is immoral, but I do not want to make it illegal. That does not mean I condone covetousness. To try to regulate covetousness would be tyrannical.

Abortions are immoral, but legislators need to be wise about what they work on to get enacted. That does not mean I condone early abortions. It means that I acknowledge the depth of mistaken majority public opinion that early abortions are okay.

A MADD Example

Fast-forward from the end of prohibition to 1980 when Candace Lightner founded Mothers Against Drunk Driving (MADD). Her daughter Cari had been walking along a quiet road on her way to a church carnival when a car swerved out of control, striking and killing her. The driver was a repeat offender.

Temperance leaders targeted drinking entirely, MADD took a more reasonable approach by targeting drunken driving alone. Law enforcement officers who were dealing with the problem on a daily basis were happy to support definitions of impairment that were easy to ascertain. Judges were ready to sentence alcohol abusers to classes on how to refrain from drunkenness and the threat of jail time was an incentive to learn.

Since then, driving impaired has become socially unacceptable and more thought is put into the use of alcohol in general. Candace Lightner did more to change our culture for the better than did millions of temperance workers. We need to put our effort into modest legislation that we can pass. We need to do what is possible instead of continually swinging for the fences and striking out. The right-fitting legislation can be the impetus for broader social change.

Anti-Family Agenda

Limited legislation and effective arguments have been used to advance the left's anti-family agenda. When I was running for the US Senate, I was invited to an interview with the Colorado Education Association for a possible endorsement. The conversation was a mutual admiration society as long as we talked about education issues. Then I was asked my opinion about homosexual teachers. I answered that it was similar to drinking. What a person did in the privacy of their own home was one thing, but a teacher should not be allowed to advocate for drinking alcoholic beverages in school.

This was not the answer they were looking for. After the meeting a participant explained that the CEA had long been a supporter of civil rights, and that issue was important to them. Is homosexuality a civil right, or is it immoral?

As I was discussing my CEA encounter with my dad, he asked how they figured homosexuality was a civil right. I said in part it is because they think homosexuals are born that way. He said, "That can't be, or there wouldn't be any." I add that if homosexuality was dominant, the continuance of our society would be endangered.

Leftists try to silence Christians by saying that to speak against an action is tantamount to spreading hate against people. A Christian view of love is willing the best for a person. Sometimes the best we can do for a person is to warn them about perilous behavior. When I was actively supporting our local drug court, several of our clients said, "The best thing that happened to me was getting arrested, because it put me in a structure to become sober."

By faith, I recognize that God's purpose in this present age is for humans to multiply. (Genesis 1). My inductive observation is that He placed a strong pleasure reward in us as an incentive to meet that purpose. Though the devil has propagated roadblocks to thwart God's purpose, his efforts have largely been unsuccessful in stopping population growth. That has not kept the devil from using people to harass and deceive others.

God created males and females for the general purpose of bringing more humans into existence. There are exceptions. Jesus and Paul never married because they had specific missions that required their full attention. My Uncle Art and Aunt Joanne were an effective missionary team and that was aided by their choice not to have children. People should seek God's guidance concerning marriage and children.

It is said that we cannot afford children. If we cared about God's purpose for us, we would invest more in children and less in weddings, abortions, hot cars, recreation vehicles, the latest phone, and eating out. It is not that we cannot afford children. Rather, it is a desire to spend more on things that bring us immediate pleasure, and don't require responsibility.

Homosexuality is frowned upon by Bible believers because it appears to run counter to the general purpose of male/female creation. The Apostle Paul called it an unnatural abomination. Evidently, he did not think it was a civil right. An interesting phenomenon is that there are evangelical conservatives and LGBTQ conservatives in the Republican Party. The reason for that may be that people in both groups desire peace. Most are not interested in parading down streets demanding to be recognized.

Though Evangelicals view homosexuality as a sin, we have not been organizing campaigns to say so. Jesus is a friend of sinners (Matthew 9:11-19). And his followers need to be also. Gluttony is a sin also. Americans do not seek to punish gluttons, even though there is a self-indulgent seeking of pleasure at the expense of health—something which the practice shares with homosexuality. All sinners will receive a just reward from our Creator. We do not have a government that deals with every sin. Rather than majoring on the minors, our government should major on the majors. Wise legislation is one way to further justice. Civil leadership is another way.

Consider the following job description of a civil activist whose role is to protect human life:

A Civil Activist's Job Description
Job Goal: to Protect Human Life

1. Humbly listen to the greatest legitimate concerns of those who want legal protection for women. Be merciful to those who have had or want to have abortions.

2. Develop the aspirations of those of us who want to have an abortion-free society while accepting political reality. We are not going to stop pre-pregnancy birth control, so we need to avoid conversations that generate undue fear on

the part of people who are uncomfortable with government intrusion into the bedroom.

3. Encourage people to think for themselves by presenting them with truthful information. Consider including abortion in the legal framework which includes child abuse and neglect. Our society has decided to restrict parents from harming their offspring, even in their own home. A child should be entitled to a safe home for its first nine months just like they are for the next 18 years of their lives.

4. Consider the talents of each individual member of the pro-life cause and how they might best contribute to anti-abortion organizations. Do everything which we can to enhance the lives of the unborn and parents, as well as those who suffer from miscarriages and/or stillbirths.

5. Expect participation in some form by every Bible-believing Christian to help reduce the number of abortions in their communities and spheres of influence, including being open to opportunities to serve in Pregnancy Resource Centers, Boards of Health, and in political parties.
6. Target the distribution of resources entrusted to you toward the needs of those who are contributing their efforts to the pro-life cause.
7. Establish a mission vision for a society where every mother, every father, and every child in every state is supported to live life to the fullest.

Chapter 9

The Political Climate

In the 1970s the environment was not an issue that divided Democrats and Republicans. A Republican administration and Democratic Congress passed the Environmental Protection Act. Environmentalists and conservationists have since moved in different directions. Many environmentalists have turned their concern for the planet into a quasi-religion including rituals (recycling) and hypocrisy (using huge amounts of resources to further their agenda). The religious environmentalists have captured the heart of the leftist movement and the Democratic party.

Adherents are strongly committed to their cause.

Conservationists gained control of the Republican Party and have become adamantly against more environmental legislation. They have reduced regulations on energy producers. The leftists' desire for more government and conservatives' desire for limited government were illustrated in positions taken on the Green New Deal—a radical approach to environmentalism which was spawned in the European Union and proposed in the US Congress where legislation failed to gain traction. A legitimate question becomes: Is science driving politics or is politics driving science?

I will do my best to discuss the matter civilly.

What About Climate Change?

My doctoral work is in Public Policy and Administration so I would like to address this issue primarily from a political standpoint and then give a layman's opinion on the physical science of climate change. I will begin with the politics of grants. When I was a county commissioner, I wrote grant applications that brought in almost $2 million to the county for road improvements. I wrote a several hundred-thousand-dollar grant for the Town of Cedaredge for improvements to its Main Street, and I was also a part of non-profit organization teams who secured large grants.

The first step in successful grant writing is finding an entity that has the funding and desire to offer grants. As an example, the Environmental Protection Agency (EPA) has a budget of $8 billion with over $4 billion dished out in grants. I do not intend to criticize the EPA, in particular. My goal is to illustrate what happens in general in the grant writing and awarding process. Much of the EPA grant money is for assisting local governments in clean water projects. I agree with that use of public funds. Much also goes to environmental research. It stands to reason that, if an entity offers grants to study the effects of carbon dioxide but does not fund grants to study the effects of water vapor, I will write a grant to study carbon dioxide, not water vapor. One way that politics drives science is by selective funding.

Another interaction of politics and science is more subtle, and it relates to the concept of need. Establishing need is a critical part of grant writing. If I was trying to show the need for my client to have a research grant to study carbon dioxide, I would be selective in my facts. I would write that pre-industrial levels of carbon dioxide were about 280 parts per million by volume (ppmv) and emphasize that current levels are greater than 400 ppmv. That sounds like a large increase. To make my point, I would avoid writing the figures as fractions, 280/1,000,000 and 400/1,000,000, because that does not look like as much. I would not mention that carbon dioxide makes up only .04 percent of the dry atmosphere or that, when you figure in particulate and water vapor, then CO_2 atmospheric content is less than .04 percent.

When I was teaching high school math, I would occasionally take an informal poll by asking what percentage of the atmosphere is made up of carbon dioxide. The most common answer was 75 percent followed by 50 percent, 25 percent, and then 4 percent. I suspect those numbers are inflated in proportion to the hype students have encountered on the effect of carbon dioxide. In my theoretical grant writing exercise begun in the paragraph above, I would not use the .04 percent figure because it is 100 times less than the 4 percent opinion that appears to be a common misconception among those who are mildly informed. The real figure is more like .0004. It is difficult to imagine that small amount of the atmosphere is going to lead to humanity's ruin. However, respected researchers have found that CO_2 is increasing (Keeling and Piper, 2001).

Researcher Charles Keeling began measuring the amount of atmospheric CO_2 from the north slope of Hawaii's big island volcano at the Mauna Loa Observatory on March 29, 1958. Keeling found that CO_2 levels varied during the day and night and also varied from season to season. Each year the amount of CO_2 increased. A lifetime of collecting data did not change those initial findings as he tried to increasingly characterize sources and sinks (that is, reductions) of atmospheric CO_2. In his analysis of data collected from 1978 to 2000, Keeling found that the terrestrial biosphere had sinks that were increasing. In other words, plant life in the regions where most of us live were removing substantial amounts of CO_2 from the atmosphere. Keeling also found that CO_2 was increasing in the polar and tropical regions (where fewer humans live). Some of Keeling's major work was funded by grants from the US National Aeronautics and Space Administration, US National Science Foundation, and the US Department of Energy, along with funding from the Scripps Institution of Oceanography.

It was a huge jump from the findings of Keeling, which I accept, to the panic, which I reject, over increases in carbon dioxide. A majority of scientists may think that people burning fossil fuels has caused an increase in airborne carbon dioxide which has led to global warming, but I doubt that a majority of scientists think this fact threatens the human species with extinction.

The Green New Deal

Representative Alexandria Ocasio-Cortez submitted a resolution to Congress in 2019 to recognize the duty of the Federal Government to create a Green New Deal. The resolution begins by referring to the October 2018 "Special Report on Global Warming of 1.5° C" by the Intergovernmental Panel on Climate Change and the November 2018 Fourth National Assessment report. This report says that human activity is the dominant cause of climate change which includes causing sea levels to rise, increases in wildfires, severe storms, droughts, and other extreme weather events that threaten human life. It says to avoid furtherance of these and other calamities, human sources of greenhouse gases must be reduced by 40 to 60 percent from 2010 levels by 2050. To achieve this target, 100 percent of the power demand in the United States is to be through clean, renewable, and zero-emission energy sources. In other words, we must stop emitting carbon dioxide that comes from using fossil fuels as a source of energy.

Leftist Democratic leaders have spoken in favor of the Green New Deal, which is a catch-all for their agenda. Republicans are concerned that such drastic action would unnecessarily harm our economy. One hundred Democratic Congressmen co-sponsored the Green New Deal. Every Republican Senator voted against it. John Feffer, director of Foreign Policy in Focus, said (2019) that the Green New Deal will not come through ordinary parliamentary and congressional procedure. It must come through a "more basic form of democracy" which he describes as people in the streets in actions like school strikes and coal mine blockades. He said this kind of pressure could be used by progressive legislatures to coerce everyone into preserving the global commons.

There are three possible responses to Feffer and other leftist radicals. They are essentially the same as the responses I outlined in chapter one as possible responses to the uncivil position of Clinton/Alinsky and their political heirs. 1) We can give in. 2) We can use uncivil tactics to try to overcome the left. 3) We can recognize the American desire for law and order, resist coercion, and proceed in a civil manner to win the people to our side. We should listen to the environmentalists with a critical, yet fair, mindset and chart a reasonable course of action.

The COVID crisis provided a perfect experiment to test the effects of reducing our use of fossil fuels. Instead of reporting data, some advocates of reducing carbon dioxide emissions say that the results of the COVID reductions will not be known for decades. That apologetic gives me greater sympathy for the skeptic's criticism that all the reported effects of carbon dioxide are within natural variance and therefore do not prove that climate change is caused by people.

A Modest Study of Temperatures

Since I could not find articles comparing daily temperatures in 2020 with previous averages, I started making tallies myself. I found the average daily temperature highs and lows from 1981–2010 in January and in April for four cities: Atlanta, Denver, New York, and Seattle. I chose January because it was just before the COVID crisis and April because then the shutdown was in full swing. I also found the actual 2020 daily high and low temperatures for January and April. I totaled the number of days in the two months where the 2020 temperatures were above average. There were less days above average in April than there were in January for all four cities, which is what would be expected if reducing carbon emissions reduces temperature.

The total number of days with temperature reductions was:

Denver   28
New York   22
Atlanta   16
Seattle   3

The average relative humidity for the time-period January through April was just the opposite:

Seattle   75%
Atlanta   65%
New York   59%
Denver   53%

Denver had the greatest average temperature change. Perhaps that is because of its low humidity. Seattle had the least change. Perhaps that is because of its high humidity. Atlanta is the highest city east of the Mississippi River. If elevation was a huge factor, then it should have come closer to Denver in temperature change. Instead, with its 65% humidity it ranked closer to Seattle.

New York was a close second to Denver in average temperature change and was also second from the least in humidity. The reduction in using fossil fuels could also have been a factor. Friends tell me that New York is generally going full tilt 24 hours a day/seven days a week. When the virus hit them hard the city almost completely shut down. From the air, Denver looks like a bunch of ants in constant movement. Cutting down on burning fossil fuels might lower temperatures in New York and Denver, but it is not as big a factor as humidity.

It appears that if we parked every car in the world, the temperature in Seattle would not change much. I like a variety of temperatures, so I am not intending to move to Seattle or the Southeast any time soon. I see no need to get on board with the drastic elements of the Green New Deal.

I realize that this was an amateurish study, but it tells me enough to look beyond carbon dioxide for solutions. We need more studies that identify what we humans can do with water vapor to improve our environment. Water vapor accounts for about 90 percent of the atmosphere's greenhouse effect. Water vapor has both cooling and warming properties. It makes cold nights less cold and hot days less hot. This leveling effect is what we need to reduce climate extremes. There is much we can do to increase water vapor while being productive. For example, scientifically planting the right crops at the right time, and informed use of irrigation.

Six Swedish scientists reported several examples of human modification of water vapor flows. As examples: Irrigated croplands in a converted steppe in Colorado increased vapor flows by 120 percent, contributing to higher precipitation and lower temperature. Significant vapor flows from irrigation also occur in central Asia, the central and western United States, southern Europe and north-central Chile. Large-scale deforestation in Australia caused a 10 percent decrease in vapor flows, which in turn reduced viable farming. Globally, deforestation has reduced vapor flows by 4 percent of the total vapor flow from the land surface, which is coincidentally about the same amount as the four percent that irrigation contributes to increasing vapor flow (Gordon, 2005).

In the Western United States, we have planted many more trees than we have harvested and that has resulted in less desert. The desert is a place of extreme temperatures. The increase in water vapor due to irrigation has moderated temperature extremes. Expanding forests is an option to decrease carbon dioxide and increase water vapor which would reduce temperature extremes. In dry areas where no irrigation is available, drought resistant shrubs or cover crops might be planted to begin reclaiming land that previous generations reduced to desert. Gordon estimates there are some 103 km² of surface land that have the potential to be forested. By my calculations that is 2,771,000 acres. That is a lot of planting to do, and it would be more efficient if done with the aid of machines powered by fossil fuels. If the leaders of numerous nations had made meaningful commitments to increasing vegetation, instead of empty promises to reduce carbon dioxide, then we would have much more stable climates today.

My Pastureland Heritage

The desire to plant and manage sustainable pastureland is a cause that runs in my family. My grandpa and grandma homesteaded a ranch on land that is now a part of Fort Carson. As a young boy during the 1930's, my dad would run a finger through the dust that had accumulated on the east window of their house. His drawing board was often renewed with a fresh coat of dust that had originated from plowed up sod in the Colorado plains. Grandpa viewed politics with a sense of humor, often teasing his staunch Republican and Democratic neighbors, but if you wanted to get him stirred up, the way to do it was to talk about land use. He would raise his voice as he proclaimed that anyone who was not a conservationist was a fool. When they later bought a ranch on the southeast edge of Black Forest, he planted alfalfa and grasses in several fields, turning land vulnerable to erosion into pasture. My grandparents were not going to contribute to the Dust Bowl.

Growing up in Black Forest when we had a hard rain, I was out building dams in little streams to capture water. In 1972, my parents sold the place in Black Forest and bought a ranch east of Cedaredge that had quality water rights. For me, irrigating near Cedaredge was like playing in the water. While living in

Black Forest, every year we would take a week or two to camp in the mountains and fish. On the new-to-us ranch near Cedaredge, we would sometimes find a fish in a ditch set. Dad would bring a fish back to the house and show everyone that it was better to be in the fiels with an irrigation shovel than by a creek with a rod and reel.

We irrigated some 200 acres of hay meadow and another hundred acres of pasture. We put up hay to feed the cows in the winter on the thick-sodded fields. As soon as we could in the spring, we would turn the cows out on irrigated and non-irrigated pastureland. We would let them go up the valley to graze on our allotment of the Grand Mesa National Forest that we leased during the summer. I figure that my family produced some one hundred thousand pounds of beef per year.

As a rancher from daylight 'till dark (and sometimes in the moonlight) I had an opportunity to observe much about weather and climate. One of the things I noticed is that clouds would travel across the desert in the southwest and when they would get over the cool green irrigated fields, they would drop their payload. Sometimes clouds would form over the ranch and shower us there or on the Mesa just above. My experience coincides with the findings of Gordon (2005) that irrigation contributes to humidity and cooling.

While I was mainly working on the family ranch, I also taught part-time and was a columnist for the Mountain Valley News. In researching an article for the paper, I was able to spend a couple of hours with a climate specialist at the National Oceanic and Atmospheric Administration in Boulder. He showed me a chart of average temperatures that was mostly flat with a few downward blips. He said the most definitive influence on climate is volcanoes and pointed to the downward spike after Tambora exploded in 1815. There was no summer in 1816 when famine followed the freezing of crops. In 1991, Pinatubo released a sulfur dioxide cloud that cooled the earth's surface for three years by as much as 1.3° F.

A Brown Cloud

Several years ago, as my wife Kristine and I drove down through the foothills into Denver we could see a brown cloud that obscured the downtown skyscrapers. We wished we could hold our breath for the week we would spend visiting her family. After front range cities adopted vehicle standards and inspections, the brown cloud went away. I wonder if the reduction in air pollution inadvertently led to higher temperatures in Colorado's front range cities.

Some say that airborne particles high in the atmosphere shade and cool the Earth while particles closer to the ground absorb the sun's rays which results in warming. Particulates from coal-fired electric generation plants may contribute to global warming. In 2018, the Department of Energy initiated funding of grants for a "CoalFIRST" program to develop small flexible coal-fired power plants with high efficiency and close to zero emissions. Critics say the grants are politically motivated. Are politically motivated grant offerings a first?

When I became a county commissioner in 2001, I supported subsidies for corn from ethanol because I thought it would extend our use of internal combustion engines to power our cars, trucks, buses, tractors, and trains. At the turn of the century, it appeared to be a fact that petroleum would become increasingly scarce. I never took the position that we would suddenly run out. I was concerned that, as production decreased, the price of gasoline would become increasingly expensive. Subsidizing the production of ethanol from corn seemed like a good idea because we could stay ahead of demand. Then I learned that it takes more fuel to make ethanol from corn than ethanol produces as a fuel. I am for farmers being fairly treated but I am not for giving them handouts that promote inefficiency. Sometimes things are labeled as renewable that are not efficient in the first place. Renewing inefficiency is not sustainable.

Any plant-based fuel releases carbon. The only difference is that the environmental pressures over time have made the older (fossilized) versions more efficient. We are currently using more fossil fuels than we should, and more judicious use would be wise, but eliminating their use is unrealistic. The call to eliminate the use of fossil fuels is a call to our youth to waste their time instead of preparing to be good stewards of the Earth and all that is on it.

The reason I am for developing pollution-free coal plants is because solar and wind generation are intermittent. When we lived in Black Forest, we had windmills that pumped water from wells into tanks for our cows to drink. Sometimes blizzards would be followed by calms that lasted for weeks. During those times we attached a belt to a pulley on the pump and to a pulley on our tractor to pump water until the wind returned. It would be nice to get a considerable amount of our electricity from windmills, but it would also be nice to have flexible coal plants for back-up. If wind was totally reliable, ranchers would not have been so eager to join Rural Electric Associations.

This little essay is not intended to be authoritative or the last word. At one time national Democrats and Republicans worked together concerning our environment. Locally, we have worked together on the Public Lands Partnership. I am hoping that some of the topics I brought up will spark some civil conversations that could lead to improving the lives of billions of us who share this planet, plus the myriads of lifeforms which we are called to manage.

Chapter 10

The Importance of Local Government

The beauty of American government is local decision making. I came to that conclusion during a lifetime of local service. Local government is my specialty both in practice and as an academic. I have served on numerous local boards, committees and collaboratives, including eight years as a Delta County Commissioner and decades as a K-12 teacher, serving at the pleasure of a local school board. I earned a Ph.D. in Public Policy and Administration with an emphasis in Leadership and Public Management. I taught courses on those subjects as well as ethics at Colorado Christian University.

I started out as an interested observer. I followed John Hawkins (Delta County Commissioner 1972-84) who was popular until his group of commissioners changed street names and addresses. I figured his loss in the next election was because of changing addresses. Soon after I took office as a commissioner, some 14 years later, I was informed by our Geography Information System (GIS) staff that we needed to change our addressing system. I told them they would have to do some heavy convincing because I would like to serve more than one term. Staff are the experts, but it is elected officials who make the most important decisions.

The Hawkins' administration was so anxious to get past the addressing ordeal that they did not assume responsibility for assigning addresses. Instead, people often made up their own address number and sometimes they got out of order. The roads were named by a grid which was fine for the flat southwest part of the county, but the rest of the county was anything but flat. To give directions to our house from Cedaredge, I had six road names to use even though the same road simply changed directions. We changed that to where my family now has to give only three road names for directions.

We kept the underlying grid. But, where roads followed a drainage, we named the road after the creek. And we named the major road on a mesa after that mesa. As we made our proposals there was quite an uproar and I started thinking about going back to teaching sooner than I had planned. I wrote letters to the editor for the two newspapers explaining why we felt we should make the changes. I received compliments on the letter/articles, the emergency and delivery people got behind it, and I was re-elected.

A thing I learned from that situation, and other controversies, is the importance of keeping people informed. The City of Delta officials at the time took an approach of strictly controlling information about what they were doing. People started mistrusting them and that trust did not come back easily. Civility tends to reduce tensions when public officials repeatedly use polite language, perhaps in monotone, and even when they are excited about such things as a road project that comes in under budget, a percent increase in sales tax revenue, or that a minority person has volunteered to serve on the economic development board.

It's All About Land Use

The reason that I got involved in local decision making was land use. As private and public land ranchers, my family's livelihood depended upon us being able to use our owned and leased land to their best productivity. I served on a local planning committee and then as an appointee to the Delta County Planning Commission. Eventually, I was elected county commissioner as a Republican dedicated to protecting people's ability to manage their property as they saw fit to do. Ultimately, I served as a commissioner for eight years.

What surprised me is that some of the same people who supported me packed the courthouse to oppose certain developments, for example, higher density suburb-like developments in rural areas.

At first, I defended the higher density subdivisions, but my position evolved. One impetus for change was a proposed subdivision close to a feedlot. I knew that it would be a short time until the new neighbors would raise so much ruckus, including lawsuits, that the feedlot would be forced out. The second thing which altered my position was a guy who hauled in a bunch of junk next to a beautifully maintained house and property. I began to settle on a principle that the existent land use had priority over a new development. I wrote the first draft of a regulation that required certain new developments to make themselves compatible with the surrounding land use.

One of my reasons for coming up with a simple regulation was because I saw other counties doggedly reject regulation until something overwhelmingly repulsive came in and then officials would rush to adopt excessive regulation, often harming agriculture. Gunnison County, our neighbor to the east, had a land use regulation which was the size of the Denver phone book. By adopting this regulation when we did, it in effect zoned most of the county as agricultural and made newer developments adjust to it.

Another reason for coming up with a regulation was to get some things hashed out so that people knew what the expectations were going to be and so they did not waste money on an investment that was not going to fly. Wise regulation can encourage sound development while avoiding unnecessary conflict.

For the most part during my time as a commissioner, I preferred asking to telling. During one commissioner meeting we were discussing complaints about how a man had strewn mobile home sections all over his property next to Highway 92. As he sat across from me, I asked if he could at least move them together, so they looked better. In the back of our meeting room his wife shouted, "Yes!" The man chuckled and then later placed the mobile homes in an orderly fashion, and we received no more complaints. Imagine how that conversation would have gone with a federal bureaucrat who had no accountability to the people his decisions affected. So long as we have private property supported by local government, we will not be subject to a Stalin-like tyrant. When a central government owns all the land, the people are doomed to be its servants. Local officials band together to keep federal land use policy to a minimum, thus heading off the possibility of a dictator.

Land use regulation in the United States is almost as varied as the landscapes themselves. We have a National Park System that preserves the most scenic places for us to visit and enjoy. The Forest Service manages its public lands to have a balance among uses that foster sustainable productivity including recreation. The Bureau of Land Management has been managed to facilitate energy development and extraction of materials necessary for production. State and local governments set aside land from development for recreation. Almost every American has the opportunity to enjoy public and private lands. County governments facilitate property ownership through Treasurer, Assessor, and Clerks offices.

My high school social studies teacher and some of my political science professors at Colorado State University said that democracy is less efficient than dictatorship. I disagree. When discussing efficiency, we should not just consider how much we are spending but how much we are spending in relation to how much we are producing. The former Soviet Union spent less on its top-down approach to governance, but they could not keep up with the overwhelming productivity of the United States.

The American system of governance allows everyone the opportunity to find a place of service. Local governments in America handle a myriad of needs: K-12 education, land use planning, economic development, hospitals, public health, waste management, domestic water, irrigation water, cemetery maintenance, recreation, county fairs, building inspection, and maintaining streets, for example, but none are more critical than law enforcement and emergency management. If you have a burglar or a fire you do not want to call someone in Washington, D.C. You want someone in your neighborhood to respond.

George W. Bush received so much criticism over his response to Hurricane Katrina that it tanked his popularity. However, the slow response to that disaster was primarily a failure of local governments, especially the city of New Orleans. The suffering of so many in the wake of Katrina illustrates the importance of doing it right.

Lightning Strikes

Lightning hit a huge old juniper tree a few hundred yards from our neighbor John's house. A fire smoldered in the dusty interior of the tree until the wind came up a few days later. Then the tree burst into flames and exploded, igniting half a dozen other junipers. John called the Cedaredge Fire Department.

While the crew got after the fire, the chief called the Hotchkiss Fire Department and the Delta County Sheriff who serves as the County Fire Marshall. The Sheriff's office set up a headquarters and traffic control, while the Sheriff called the Colorado State Forest Service and a local crop duster to start spraying fire retardant on John's and his brother Roy's houses. A strong wind quickly pushed the fire up the Currant Creek drainage past the abandoned McGruder Coal Mine. The Colorado State Forester asked for a federal hotshot crew to fight the wildfire while the Cedaredge and Hotchkiss fire departments concentrated on protecting the houses.

At each stage there was a formal transfer of responsibility: from Cedaredge to the Sheriff, from the Sheriff to the State, from the State to the federal hot shots. Each transfer took minutes, and the hot shot crew was working within hours. Federal helicopters carried water from a nearby pond to strategic locations to limit the fire. The McGruder fire was contained within a day, and no houses were lost.

Hurricane Katrina was many times worse than the McGruder Fire. The local response was also many times worse. They could not even get the traffic control right. Even worse, federal money which had been allocated to strengthen levees was squandered. When local governments do not respond quickly and call for appropriate resources, the situation becomes much worse.

A year after the Katrina disaster, I attended a National Association of Counties meeting. While there, I asked an Alabama County Commissioner how significant the help of churches had been in the recovery. Thousands of churches went to help for weeks. He said the assistance was fantastic and immeasurable. We never heard about their huge contribution because it does not fit the narrative of the mainstream media. Their narrative was to blame Bush. On a more positive note, natural disaster response has gotten better especially when it starts with local government.

Insights

Another good thing about local government is that it provides insight into state and national politics. Bill Owens was a competent Colorado governor from 2001-09 who, among other things, widened Interstate-25 and supported practical pro-life measures. However, in response to a media uproar to "close the gun show loophole" Governor Owens signed legislation to require background checks at gun shows. This requirement shut down many gun shows. Those shows had been a convenient way for individuals who were interested in selling a firearm to meet with individuals who were interested in purchasing what were generally collector items. This was safer than putting an ad in the paper. Occasionally, I would go with my dad who was a regular at the Grand Junction gun show. Dad looked for collectable pocketknives and visited with people who had similar interests. I would not describe Dad, or those he visited with, as dangers to society.

As much as I agree that Governor Owens and the legislature made the wrong decision regarding gun show background checks, I still think he did a great job overall. Yet some Republicans thought he was not a true conservative because of that one issue. During Owens' terms, Lieutenant Governor Jane Norton was regarded by many who knew her as one of the most competent public officials in Colorado. Because many Republicans associated Norton with Owens, they would not support her when she ran for the US Senate. Instead, they chose a staunch libertarian candidate who did not get elected in the Colorado statewide election, because Democratic candidate Michael Bennet seemed less radical to swing voters.

When President Trump appointed Judge Neil Gorsuch to the Supreme Court, I wrote a letter to Senator Bennet encouraging him to vote to confirm a fellow Coloradoan. I think he seriously considered it, but as Bennet looked at the big picture of furthering his liberal agenda, he voted against confirmation. In this case, the leaders of liberal Democrats in Colorado showed themselves to be more politically savvy than those leading conservative Republicans.

Bennet was appointed to the Senate Judicial Committee where he stood by as Chairman Charles Grassley asked Dr. Christine Blaséy Ford if she knew that the committee had been willing to go to California to meet with her privately. She said her lawyers had not told her that. Evidently, they and Senator Dianne Feinstein, who recommended the attorneys, were more interested in embarrassing Judge Brett Kavanaugh than they were in protecting Dr. Ford. Senator Bennet appeared to condone Feinstein's impropriety and voted against the confirmation of Kavanaugh.

The Christian Vote

In a pamphlet on behalf of the Family Research Council, David Closson (2020) tried to convince Christians to vote. I am not going to spend much time arguing for Christians to vote. Voting ought to be a given. I heard a missionary on furlough say he did not understand why church people in America would not vote for the lesser of two evils. What is the alternative? Not voting? Apparently, for many, it is.

Some say, "I want to send a message." The messages they are sending may not be the messages they intend to send. Rather than a stance for Christian principles, their message may be that they are content with the election of increasingly uncivil power seekers. The real message is, "I will not oppose the devil's efforts to shut down evangelism." For others the message may be that leisure is their most important activity without regard for the country or those who sacrificed to give us the opportunity to make choices.

Besides voting, a conservative Christian should seriously consider becoming involved in a political party. This greatly increases a person's influence with a small investment of time. I would be happy if Christians formed the majority in both major parties and the smaller parties. In Colorado, a person can take a few minutes to cast a mail-in ballot in a primary for presidential candidates once every four years. A person can go to a caucus meeting one evening every two years to elect delegates to the county convention and make nominations for state representatives to the legislature and to the state convention. If a person lives in a part of the state furthest away from the state convention, they are still only going to be out two days every two years counting travel and the convention. If Christians had invested an evening, a morning, and two days in the space of two years they could have helped elect Jane Norton to the Senate and that body would have been more civil. When she was Lieutenant Governor, she led a Bible study in the state capital. How great would it have been to have a senator whose goal was to apply the Bible to governance? How nice would it be if most of those attending party conventions had both an appreciation for the Bible and an appreciation for politics?

Start Local

To best understand the American political system, a person should start at the local level. We used to call it "paying your dues." We need representatives in Congress and the state houses from a variety of careers and professional expertise, and with practical knowledge of governance. Most local political offices are part-time, so a person can develop expertise in a career and in politics at the same time. Recently, Republicans have pushed candidates with no political experience, which has been a disservice to our party and the country. To adequately understand what it means to have self-government, a person needs to understand local government. Sending novice politicians to D.C. will not drain a swamp. Sending savvy and civil patriots to D.C. will channel power through local governments back to the people.

Follow the Money

Conservatives must step up our contributions to elections because that is a crucial aspect of governance in America. Campaign managers must provide workers with the resources they need to carry out their tasks. Money is often the deciding factor in state office and Congressional campaigns. For a time, I would not accept the truth that money is a deciding factor, and that oversight prevented me from doing as well as I could have. Lawmakers have tried to limit the amount of money going into campaigns. In 2020 the maximum contribution for a couple to a presidential campaign was $5,600. However, people find ways around the limits, for example, by forming Political Action Committees (PACs) that have no contribution limits.

Or some can get very creative, such as Mark Zuckerberg who poured $350 million into elections through his non-profit Center for Tech and Civic Life (CTCL) which was run by former Obama staffers to provide grants to local governments to get out the vote. Zuckerberg claimed the grants went to Republican as well as Democratic jurisdictions. However, David Bossie (2022) pointed out that Democrats received more money, and also that more of that money was directed at registering Democratic voters and getting them to the polls. Since 2020, 28 states have banned so-called Zuckerbucks. Congresswoman Claudia Tenney introduced the End Zuckerbucks Act to prohibit charitable tax-exempt organizations from providing direct funding to official election organizations.

Registering people who will likely vote your way is a part of the "ground game" that is the most cost-effective aspect of campaigning. Zuckerberg crossed the line of ethical fairness, but it is fair to have a ground game without paying officials. The Faith and Freedom Coalition and other conservative organizations showed us how to do it right in the 2020 Virginia governor's race. Virginia should be our model in Colorado and other states.

Contributing to political campaigns does not mean that everyone must do the same thing. Some outgoing people might be good at knocking on doors. A quiet techy person might help with sharing messages through social media. I had a television director and producer who donated their time and equipment to develop material for my website, and they produced a result which was envied by my wealthy opponent. If we are not willing to put time, energy and money into winning campaigns then we should question whether or not our hearts are really into helping our government civilly expand opportunity and freedom.

God Is God

When people get a taste for power, at any level, we must be careful not to exaggerate our importance. The COVID virus showed how quickly an economy can be brought to a halt and how precious a simple breath can be. We can do nothing by ourselves. The only time we accomplish anything is as God works through us. We need to acknowledge that God is God, and we are not; then accept His direction as a light in the darkness.

I have heard liberals question why conservatives, and particularly Evangelicals, have been supportive of Trump when he has engaged in behavior that does not appear consistent with our values. It is a legitimate question with a complex answer. Part of the reason is found in the story of the lazy boy who cried wolf. The third time that he cried wolf, the villagers paid no attention. The Democrats have unmercifully and persistently gone after Trump for petty things which appeared obviously partisan. They have cried wolf so often that conservative Christians have been reluctant to join the campaign to make Trump look bad. While critics have accused Trump of lying, they themselves have tried to skew peoples' impression of him by not telling the whole truth.

The qualification of being morally beyond reproach is thought by some to be more a qualification for a pastor than for a president. The courage to be a champion to appoint pro-life judges and move the American Embassy to Jerusalem are of more concern than reports of decades-old sexual indiscretions. Those who change from a life of sin to being upright are heroes in the Evangelical world—although Trump does not fit that model precisely. So far, it has been purported that Trump's wrongdoing is mostly in the past, when he was cozy with establishment Democrats. Part of the virulence of the attacks on Trump are because he turned on them. Because he knew how establishment Democrats and Republicans operate, he was effective in countering their liberal agenda.

Some people think the party system in this country is the cause of incivility. It is not the system; it is the nature of people who are the problem. If you do not like the morals of our leaders, then get involved and be the type of politician you would like others to be.

Chapter 11

Election Integrity

The revolutionary Americans not only rejected having a king, they also rejected inherited leadership. They instead pursued elections. We have generally benefited by having more competent people elected to positions of authority over having inherited their positions. The problems we have had stem from good people not participating in the voting process. As good people challenged the Daley machine in Chicago and Jim Crow laws in the South, we have kept fraud to practically insignificant numbers. By the time of Jimmy Carter's Presidency, the American election system was so well respected that he sent experts to other countries to help them with sound processes. However, more recently the validity of US Presidential elections has been questioned.

In her book *What Happened?* Hillary Clinton said that Trump colluded with the Russians to steal the 2016 election (Clinton, 2017). In 2019, she was still insisting that he stole the election. In Inglewood, California, during a speaking tour with former president Bill Clinton she said, "I think it's also critical to understand that, as I've been telling candidates who have come to see me, you can run the best campaign, you can even become the nominee, and you can have the election stolen from you," (Reynolds, 2019). Clinton had spent decades of preparation to become the first woman president. From her perspective the only way she could have been denied the presidency was if it had been stolen from her.

Clinton may have been so insistent there was evidence that Trump colluded with the Russians because her campaign paid for the fake evidence. During the trial of Michael

Sussman, which was brought by Special Prosecutor John Durham in 2022, former Clinton campaign general counsel Marc Elias testified that he hired the opposition research firm Fusion GPS on behalf of the Clinton campaign. Clinton campaign manager Robby Mook took the stand and testified that Hillary Clinton herself approved the dissemination of materials alleging a covert communications channel between the Trump Organization and the Russian Alfa Bank, despite campaign officials questioning the legitimacy of the claim. The Federal Elections Commission fined the Democratic National Committee and Hillary for America for failure to accurately disclose the purpose of the payments to Fusion GPS through Elias and his firm Perkins Cole (Calvin, 2022).

Devin Nunes, Chairman, of the House Intelligence Committee, found that the fake evidence compiled by former British spy Christopher Steele was preposterous, yet it was used by the FBI to get a warrant to surveil Trump campaign volunteer Carter Page.

Attorney General James Comey was often quoted as saying the Steele Dossier was salacious and unverifiable and that is why his office did not make it available to the public. The Clinton campaign had released the material as a late campaign surprise in an effort to secure the election. It was not enough to overcome a lackluster campaign on her part, where she appeared to be ailing.

After an exhaustive investigation, the Mueller Commission found no incriminating evidence of anyone in Trump's campaign colluding with the Russians. Attorney General William Barr summarized the Mueller report as showing there was no collusion and no evidence of interference.

Even if some Russians and the Trump campaign had come to some agreement on campaign strategy, that would not have constituted stealing the election. My experience in campaigns and local government makes me skeptical about any claims of large-scale fraud. I reject the idea that the Russians, the Chinese, Democrats, Republicans, or anyone one else could steal a US presidential election. It is not that I do not believe there are those who want to control our elections. It is that the structure of our elections system is virtually impervious to large-scale fraud. It would even be difficult to steal a local election. I was a candidate in one national and three local elections, so I had stakes in the results as I carefully observed the process. I have no doubt that I, in fact, won the elections which election officials said I won, and I lost the elections that election officials said I lost.

Decentralization Versus Fraud

The election process in the United States is highly decentralized, and that is a good thing to prevent major fraud. The United States administers elections through more than three thousand counties divided into 175,441 precincts or precinct equivalents in the states plus D.C. and 1,492 in overseas US territories (Election Assistance, 2020). Each precinct is managed by locals whose purpose is to make sure everyone has the opportunity to register and to vote while also assuring that those not entitled are not allowed to vote. Ballots and voting machines are always under the custody of election officials or locked in a secure room.

People may not realize that county clerks oversee the design and printing of ballots to account for all the races unique to a particular jurisdiction. For example, each city and town will have separate unique ballots, plus some of dozens of special districts may also have candidates and\or issues that other people in other districts do not get to vote on. That makes it impossible for a ballot counting manufacturer to preset the percentage of votes years in advance. Sometimes the Republican candidate wins a coin toss and gets top line on the ballot and sometimes the Democratic candidate gets top line. That is another reason that ballot counting machine manufacturers cannot steal an election.

Examples from the 2020 election help to show why claims of theft in both 2016 and 2020 were dubious. In October of 2020, Antrim County, Michigan election officials changed three ballot designs to account for local contests after the initial designs had already been loaded onto the memory cards that configure the ballot scanners. In their haste, they did not reconfigure all the memory cards and errors resulted. Antrim County became the centerpiece of claims of election fraud. Some claimed that voting machines were pre-programmed to skew the election results away from Trump, but the numerous ballot styles changing unpredictably made that impossible. Voting machine computers are not like our laptops or desktops that are good for various tasks including connecting with the internet. Voting machine computers are more like those in our cars that are designed for specific tasks and are generally not capable of internet connection. If machines are internet capable, that function is to be turned off during the collection and processing of ballots. In Colorado, both a state official and a county official must be present to enter passwords in order to access the internet on those computers that are internet capable.

Unofficial Versus Official Results

Another thing that may be overlooked is the difference between unofficial and official results. The results that are first carried by the news media are mostly unofficial results. Local election officials go through a series of audits to discover and correct any errors. On November 4, 2020, the Antrim clerk reported unofficial results of 7769 votes for Biden and 4509 votes for Trump. After going through the machine audits, it was officially reported on November 21 that Biden had 5960 votes and Trump had 9748.

A state audit, including a hand count, confirmed the official results. Although machines are used for counting, paper ballots or receipts and careful hand counts are still the basis for the final word in most states and should be in all of them. Close elections are automatically recounted. If an election is not close, the candidate must pay for the recount. A 54-page document was prepared for the state of Michigan by J. Alex Haldeman, Ph.D. detailing the results of the state's audits of Antrim County. The state's results were the same as the official results certified by their county commissioners. The bottom line is that Trump received 9,748 votes from Antrim County, yet Trump was still maintaining in late December of 2020 that 8,000 votes were stolen from him there.

Soon after the 2020 election, my friends sent me links to websites purporting that the election was stolen, and Antrim County was prime evidence. One of the links was to a YouTube production by Mike Lindell (the My Pillow CEO). It was later blocked, and I wish it wasn't so my readers could confirm what I am saying. Lindell's video began with a background graphic that showed little squares coming into parts of the US from various places, but especially from China to Georgia. It reminded me of getting a cat to chase light reflected from a watch or the misdirection of a salesman using irrelevant demonstrations to peddle his wares. Paper ballots are the foundation for election counts and I doubt paper ballots were flown in from China nor produced in their huge embassy in D.C.—let alone paper ballots which would account for numerous ballot styles and containing names of actual registered voters who had not voted. Double votes would have been caught.

Lindell's guests talked about data dumps at specific times that supposedly changed the course of the election from Trump's favor to Biden's. Different jurisdictions have different habits that influence the timing of posting results. Television election experts reported which counties leaned which way and it was no surprise to long-time observers that later reporting Atlanta precincts gave Biden a narrow win in Georgia. In my own experience during my congressional race in 2008, I was ahead as smaller conservative counties reported but I was not surprised when the Democratic stronghold of Pueblo finally reported enough votes to overcome my early lead.

The other county which received major attention in 2020 was Mesa County, Colorado, next door neighbor to my Delta County. One of the stolen election experts, Jeffrey O'Donnel, said that Mesa County was the door to him seeing the nature of massive election fraud. In that case his analysis was flawed. O'Donnel sent a letter to the Mesa County Board of County Commissioners (BoCC) saying that it was not county staff but rather Dominion

Voting Systems or an unknown party via the internet that caused irregularities. The report prompted District Attorney Dan Rubinstein to investigate the causes of discrepancies in the voting count. Rubinstein reported to the BoCC that elections manager Sandra Brown had errored in adjudicating ballots twice. The DAs office had no evidence that Sarah Brown's actions involved ill intent or a criminal offense. They had no evidence that it affected the official results at all (Woodbrey, 2022).

The two high profile election errors in Antrim and Mesa counties were the centerpieces of supposed evidence of election fraud and their supposedly suspect results were projected as percentages of fraud for the whole country. In the now-suppressed video, participants pointed to graphs which displayed the same peaks and valleys throughout the counties whose election data they analyzed. All the graphs were shiny stuff to distract from the fact that errors were corrected between the unofficial count and the official count. Vote counting machines are a convenience. Authorized trained people counting paper ballots has remained the final test to ensure accuracy in Georgia, Michigan, Arizona, Colorado and almost all other states.

Litigation

Eventually, Fox News abandoned their commentators' claims that Dominion Voting Systems were rigged against Trump, but not soon enough to avoid a lawsuit in which Fox agreed to pay some $787 million to Dominion to settle a defamation suit. Is it any wonder that Rupert Murdock soured on Trump supporters as a reliable source of election information?

Rudy Giuliani had a small army of lawyers preparing lawsuits likely even before Trump proclaimed that the election was stolen. I read through some of the lawsuits brought to challenge the 2020 presidential election. There was one major problem. The plaintiffs failed to present one instance of voter fraud in jurisdictions where they filed. Texas attorney, Sydney Powell, who allegedly engaged in illegal efforts to access voting equipment in Georgia and elsewhere, got into the act, appearing on the Lou Dobbs show to say that she had plenty of evidence of voter fraud. When she was unable to produce any, she was no longer asked to be a special guest on Fox channels. Her lawsuit contained spelling errors and was so poorly written that the judge was upset with her for wasting the court's time. Powell was not wasting her own time as she raised more than 16.4 million dollars for her organization Defending the Republic which she claimed was to protect election integrity (Swaine & Brown, 2020).

A Summary of Voter Fraud

I looked through a summary of voter fraud that was compiled by the Heritage Foundation. For 2020, there were 16 instances of fraud that were not in swing states. The only conviction in a swing state was of Randy Jumper who pleaded guilty to attempting to vote twice—once by mail in Pima County, Arizona where he had moved from and once in person in Washoe County, Nevada where he lived at the time of the election. The Arizona Secretary of State's office had referred the instance to the Arizona Attorney General's office who prosecuted the case. A judge sentenced Jumper to three years of probation, a $5,000 fine and 300 hours of community service (AZAG, 2022).

As a county commissioner I had to certify the results of ballot counts in Delta County for two presidential elections. I observed the whole process from registration to checking IDs at polling places to mailing in a ballot myself that required my signature and was checked by an elections officer. Even with my responsibility, I could not just walk into the lockable room where the ballots and machines were used and stored. Nor could the county clerk or staff go into that room by themselves. There always had to be at least one authorized and trained representative from the Republicans, one from the Democrats and one clerk employee.

People should not expect to barge in where ballots are being officially counted when they have not gone through a process of authorization beginning several months before the election. While we are standing to honor those who serve our country, we should give a shout out to those patriotic citizens who donate their time to know the election process intimately and then see that it is carried out. May God bless you. If you want to observe elections, take the time to do it right—decently and in order. President Trump and Secretary Clinton alienated tens of thousands of patriotic election workers when they claimed their elections were stolen.

Close to Home

An important aspect of American practice is that elections are conducted by local officials. It works well for people close to home to do the work so that locals can observe the process and the results. It is fine for state and national officials to provide oversight and accountability in monitoring elections. However, it would cost the federal government a tremendous amount of money to administer elections as well as they are conducted now, which is partly by volunteers. A federal administration of elections would run counter to the very principle the founders set up of individual control first, local government second, then state government, and, last of all, federal government.

The Democrats introduced House Bill 1 into Congress in 2022 which was intended to fix our election system. We should diligently resist efforts to fix a system that is not broken. We do not want fixed elections. The mechanics of our American electoral system are sound. The lack of integrity is on the part of the people who seek to gain or retain power at any cost, led by the losers of the 2016 and 2020 presidential elections. An increase in federal control of elections is exactly what we do not need.

Kellyanne Conway said Hillary Clinton lost the 2016 election fairly and squarely, "and when she says that election was stolen from her, she's playing a dangerous game." (Wise, Justin, 5/7/19). Ned Ryan said Clinton should be embarrassed for making such outlandish claims. She ran a terrible campaign, and she bears the responsibility for her election loss

(Reynolds, 2019). Even though she was one of Trump's most loyal supporters, Conway told him that he lost his bid for re-election. Whatever Clinton said, Trump would say it louder. An assistant pastor observed his mentor's notes, "Weak point. Speak loudly." The loudness of Trump's cry that the 2020 presidential election was stolen from him is only matched by the lack of evidence in support of such a fantastic claim.

Ivanka Trump said that Attorney General Barr seemed like an honorable man, and she believed him when he told the President three times that there was nothing to the claims of widespread election fraud. As the chief law enforcement officer, the third time that Barr reported on the matter, he suggested that if Trump still believed the election was stolen, he had developed mental problems.

A Rocky Beginning

The Trump administration had a rocky beginning in 2017 but by the second year he had a team that was humming. At the State of the Union address in 2019, Republicans cheered as Trump went over their accomplishments. They had brought jobs back from China and Mexico. The low unemployment rates of minorities were cutting into their support for Democrats. Those Democrats watched soberly as Republicans cheered—a celebration highlighted by giving Rush Limbaugh the Presidential Medal of Freedom. Perhaps Trump's most important accomplishment was appointing three conscientious Supreme Court Judges. His administration had dozens of successes that strengthened America. In doing so he endeared himself to loyal followers who would not abandon him, even in the face of criminal charges.

At the time of the 2019 State of the Union Address there was only one man who could stand in the way of Trump's re-election and that was Trump himself. How could he lose? From his 2016 campaign through 2018 Trump seemed to get everything right. From 2019 on he used increasingly poor judgement.

Lou Dobbs proclaimed that Donald Trump was the greatest president ever, including George Washington. Trump accepted the accolade without credit to others or to his Creator. I thought of King Nebuchadnezzar, who congratulated himself on building a great palace in Babylon and thought he did so by his own power. He was driven out of the city and ate grass until his reason returned to him, and then he praised the Most High God, who is able to abase those who walk in pride (Daniel 4).

Trump was turned out to pasture through former Vice President Joe Biden, even though Biden appeared to be a weak candidate. Biden did not win his first debate with Trump. Trump lost it. All Trump had to do was be poised as he briefly worked some of the administration's accomplishments into answers to tough questions—questions that he should have anticipated moderator Chris Wallace would ask. Rather than listen to his competent campaign staff, Trump took the hardline approach recommended by Giuliani. In front of a nationwide audience, and especially swing voters, Trump was rude, frequently interrupting and persistently talking beyond his allotted time. Instead of touting gains in employment for minorities he called on knucklehead Proud Boys to stand back and stand by. That would not only give pause to those who were concerned about white supremacists, but also to peace-loving independents.

Conservative talk show hosts were saying that the 2020 election was the most important ever. Trump acted as if he believed it and that he was the only person who stood in the way of a Democratic take-over that he proclaimed would ruin the country. Instead of the 2016 Trump who pursued American businessmen and American labor under the banner of Make America Great Again, the 2020 campaign seemed to be Make Trump Great Again so he could retain power. Trump believed that he had put together a movement loyal to himself that was greater than any other in history. Perhaps without realizing it, Trump adopted an Alinsky-win-at-any-cost attitude. Giuliani was right with him in an all-out effort to retain power.

Despite pressure by Giuliani on some local officials to change their results, the orderly process of certifying results from local to state governments continued. The certified state results were scheduled by law to be recorded at a joint session of Congress on January 6, 2020, with Vice President Mike Pence presiding.

Attorney John Charles Eastman gave Trump and Giuliani the idea that Pence did not have to receive the official results from the states. That is one of the most un-American ideas I have ever heard of, yet Trump accepted it. Vice President Pence rejected the idea.

> Pence said, "Our Founders were deeply suspicious of consolidated power in the nation's capital and were rightly concerned with foreign interference if presidential elections were decided in the capitol. But there are those in our own party who believe that as the presiding officer over the joint session

of Congress, I possessed unilateral authority to reject electoral college votes. And I heard this week, President Trump said I had a right to 'overturn the election'. President Trump is wrong...I had no right to overturn the election" (PBS, 2021).

On December 19, 2020, President Trump announced a rally to be held January 6. Perhaps a large show of support would convince the Vice President to ignore the state submissions. On December 20, Enrique Tarrio, the founder of the Proud Boys, began planning for the event. On January 6, while President Trump was still speaking to thousands at the Ellipse, a park south of the White House, the Proud Boys were joined by Oath Keepers and a few hundred other knuckleheads who were ultimately indicted by the Department of Justice for inciting a crowd, breaching barriers, breaking windows, and harming police in an unauthorized entrance into the west side of the Capitol Building. The riot was quashed in a few hours.

After Trump finished his speech, several hundred made their way to the east side of the Capitol Building where they were let in. Some of them had permits to speak on the grounds. They left the Capitol building when they were asked to leave (Davidson, 2025). One of those who had a permit to speak was Dr. Simone Gold who was sentenced to a maximum-security prison. The Garland Justice Department pursued and jailed more than a thousand peaceful protesters. Trump rightly pardoned them, but he also pardoned those who had violently stormed the Capitol Building. The House Select Committee on January 6 made biased presentations against Trump, falsely accusing him of trying to overthrow the government. President Trump has not publicly acknowledged any responsibility for what he initiated, albeit in response to decades of liberal deconstruction of America. I have never seen anything like the recent false claims of election fraud, imprisoning peaceful protestors, or pardoning violent knuckleheads. The whole matter is a trend in the wrong direction if we are to thrive as a country. And, of course, the entire matter is decidedly uncivil.

God and Donald Trump

Prior to the 2016 election, Franklyn Graham, an American evangelist and president of Samaritan's Purse, led prayer meetings at the capitols of each of the 50 states. It occurs to me that Donald Trump was one of the answers to those prayers. As God put Trump in office, He could also take him out, and He did. When Nebuchadnezzar repented and acknowledged the power of God, God restored him to a powerful position He wanted him to have. Trump was so far down after unprecedented attacks on him that a return to office would be humanly impossible. Several speakers at the Republican convention in 2024 acknowledged God's protection from a would-be assassin's bullet. The message was not lost on President Trump. If God is for you, what does it matter who is against you? Evidently, President Trump recognizes that God is the General Manager of the Universe and that has been repentance enough that God made him President again.

How can I say that God put Trump back in office when he received 312 electoral votes based on 77,237,942 votes cast by humans compared to 226 electoral votes based on 74,946,837 votes cast by humans for Kamala Harris. That was clearly a human choice so what does God have to do with it? The answer is that God works through human choice. To Harris' credit, she did not claim that the election was stolen from her. Biden might have made that claim, but he was too feeble to get very far with the argument.

Candidate Trump corrected two of the foolish things that he did in 2020. In 2024, Trump worked hard to gain almost unanimous support from Republicans as opposed to picking a public fight with the popular Republican governor of Georgia as he did in 2020. Secondly, Trump encouraged his supporters not to use mail in voting in 2020. The

2024 campaign corrected that by encouraging supporters to vote by mail and the results were much better.

In the debates over the Electoral College versus the popular vote methods of conducting an election, the 2020 presidential election shows the value of the Electoral College system as adding layers for election accuracy. We Americans are impatient. We want results now. For most of our history we have been able to set aside our desire for immediate gratification in favor of getting things right. Nevertheless, there is a limit to patience and only votes cast on or before election day and night should be counted. California is one of eight states that legalizes late voting. In 2024, the winner of California's 13th Congressional District was not declared until a month after the election. That delay smacks of gross incompetence even beyond that of the California legislature.

If we are to survive as a civil society, Americans of strong moral character from across the country must get involved in elections. Then we can become concerned about the proper actions of those who are elected.

Chapter 12

Heavenly Government

When a person is elected to office, he/she alone gets to serve in that position. God has called each one of us to a unique office. The choice we have is whether or not to accept that position. We cannot choose for someone else, and no one else can choose for us. When we accept the call, we are chosen to be a follower of Christ. Most of the American founders recognized Christ as their King then and in the future. That was a factor in not recognizing any other man as King.

Every Sunday millions pray, "Thy Kingdom come. Thy will be done on earth as it is in heaven," (Matthew 6:10, KJV). God will answer that prayer through sending Jesus to physically return to Earth to rule His Kingdom. Those who are chosen will rule with Him. Some think that it would be heaven if we had no government. The opposite is true. The more people who accept their call, the closer we will get to a heavenly government. The more people are too proud to seek God's will, the worse our society will be.

Earlier I described seven research-based characteristics of effective leaders. Jesus exemplifies them well. As we follow His call, we will have His help to incorporate good characteristics into carrying out our responsibilities.

Jesus Establishes Justice.

One of the distressing things to see in the workplace is a boss so weak that he/she will not confront people when they are not doing their work or are being disruptive so others cannot do their work. That goes for teachers in the school setting also. To turn the other cheek has a context. There are times for strong people to strategically turn the other cheek.

There are other times when it is best to pressure others to turn away from disruptive behavior.

When people are doing good, they should be rewarded. When people are doing evil, they should be stopped. That is the essence of doing justice. It is also a call for discernment. Politicians in the San Francisco area aided Jim Jones as he used assistance to needy people to gather some 900 members into a socialist commune (Dwyer, 2012). Jones moved the group to a remote part of the Guyana rain forest. There he directed them to drink a cyanide laced fruit drink similar to Kool-Aid. We use the phrase "drinking the Kool-Aid" to describe accepting someone's propaganda which ultimately leads to our destruction.

In much of academia, social justice is our most noble cause. Much good comes from well-designed social justice projects. But social justice advocates can be prone to drink the Kool-Aid and ignore instances of socialism turned evil. Efforts toward a utopia have largely gone awry with the grandest ideas often being the worst—the former Soviet Socialists being a sobering example of a crowning "achievement."

One of the best-known Bible prophecies regards a coming dictator, popularly called the Antichrist and thought to be someone like Stalin, Hitler, or Mussolini. The book of Revelation refers to this coming ruler as the beast, probably because he will be brutal. For a while I thought the beast would be a clever Machiavellian who fools people as he sneaks into an established political position. Now I am more inclined to anticipate a brute who will strike people with fear. He will likely have sophisticated supporters, but he will be openly and terribly mean.

The guy who most exemplifies the beast was Antiochus IV, a Greek ruler who sought to Hellenize (make Greek) the people he conquered in the Middle East by force. He was particularly severe in his harassment of those who practiced Judaism. He had active Jews flogged and crucified or stoned. Antiochus occupied the Jewish Temple and called himself Epiphanes (God Manifest) saying he was Zeus incarnate. The Jews called him Epimenes (the insane one).

Epimenes had pigs sacrificed and their blood sprinkled on the altar. The prophet Daniel refers to this as the Abomination of Desolation (Daniel 11). Jesus refers to Daniel when he said to watch for the coming abomination of desolation standing in the Holy Place (Matthew 24:15). Many will drink the Kool-Aid and follow the beast. John, the author of Revelation, says there will also be a false prophet who will command people to worship the beast while he persecutes the saints.

When things look bleakest, a cavalry riding white horses with Jesus in the lead, also riding a white horse, will conquer the beast and slay the beast's army. For many days birds will gorge themselves on the flesh of those who did not hesitate to hurt others. Jesus will establish a just kingdom defined by the Bible and not by today's advocates of wokeness.

Isaiah 65:21-23 says people will build houses and live in them. People will plant orchards and eat their fruit. A just society makes it easy for people to be rewarded for their useful effort. That will be a welcome change from rewarding those who cheat. The only utopia that will be successfully established is when Christ returns to set up His Kingdom on Earth. There will be no doubt that He is God. Handel powerfully set the words of Isaiah to music, "His name shall be called, Wonderful, Counselor, the Mighty God, the Everlasting Father, the Prince of Peace" (Isaiah 9:6, KJV).

Jesus Supplies the Needs of those in Ministry

The followers of Christ are and will be a Kingdom of Priests (1 Peter 2:9). To help people relate to God, priests themselves must first and foremost have a relationship with God. Jesus provides access to God (1Timothy). Jesus provided what we need to walk with God ourselves and point others to Him. We do not just waltz into the presence of God unprepared. Revelation 5:9-10 says it is through the blood of the Lamb of God who was slain as a sacrifice for our sin that we join the Kingdom of Priests who will reign upon the earth. The crucial element is the blood of Jesus which He poured out as a sacrifice to make the ultimate payment for our transgression. The blood of Jesus makes those He chooses to become priests (Revelation 6:10). God has supplied us with the message that we are to take to others to give them access to God.

I mentioned before that when I was 14 my family started going to a Baptist mission and there I heard and responded to the gospel. There was an important context that kept us going back to hear the message. The people there displayed extraordinary friendliness and joy. How do we obtain the joy that was so attractive to us and makes us attractive to others so that they will be interested in hearing the message of salvation that enables others to walk with God?

It is not by getting a ton of money to buy beautiful things. It is just the opposite. To begin His sermon on the mount Jesus lists the characteristics of those who will receive His joy. Jesus blesses people with joy who realize their need, mourn, humble themselves, hunger for righteousness, are merciful, pure in heart and persecuted for Jesus' sake. The poor in spirit realize we are destitute without God, and they recognize the importance of setting aside anything that draws our attention away from God.

One of the surprising things to me is that Jesus has given me joy in the midst of suffering. Mourning has been a bitter/sweet experience. Knowing that the Holy Spirit will comfort me reduces my fear of suffering.

Some people who don't have a clue about the blessing that comes with owning a piece of land look down on farmers. People in agriculture own most of the private land now in America and they will in the future kingdom as well. Jesus gives the land to those of a humble mindset.

If you want to be assured that you will receive what you strive for, hunger and thirst to do things right. Jesus will make it happen for you so you can be a good example for others. In Jesus' Sermon on the Mount, he teaches us to ask forgiveness for our transgressions or trespassing over healthy boundaries. As we have mercy on those who offend us, we can have mercy shown toward us.

The Pharisees pretended to be holy to impress people. Jesus said they had their reward. Those pure in heart who truly seek God and His guidance will see God. I was surprised and delighted with the joy which Jesus gave me when others tried to harm me because of my faith.

These eight mindsets which Jesus set forth in his Sermon on the Mount are blessings that facilitate joy and will help us to be good ministers of the gospel. In seeking first Jesus' Kingdom it does not mean we have no regard for material things like food and shelter. Jesus knows we need these things and will supply all our needs according to his riches in glory (Philippians 4:19). God's provision is not meant for hoarding. As we share God's blessing with others, we expand our ministry opportunities.

When Jesus returns and the angels with Him, He will sit on His glorious throne and people from all the nations will be gathered before Him. He will separate the people into two groups, as a shepherd separates sheep from goats. To those on His right hand He will say, "Come you who are blessed of My Father, inherit the kingdom prepared for you from the foundation of the world. For I was hungry, and you gave me something to eat; I was thirsty, and you gave me something to drink; I was a stranger, and you invited Me in; naked and you clothed Me; I was sick, and you visited Me; I was in prison, and you came to Me" (Matthew 25:31-46).

To those on the left, Jesus will say to depart into the fire prepared for the devil, because even though they claimed to know Him, they did not know Him as shown by their lack of providing for the needs of others, which is evidently of great importance to God.

Jesus Expects Meaningful Participation

Two of Jesus' parables exemplify His desire for all to participate in carrying out their responsibilities (Matthew 25:14-30; Luke (19:11-27). In both stories outlined in the foregoing scriptures, the Master provided servants with various sums of money, perhaps years of wages. After a long time, the Master returned to have the servants give an accounting. In the story recorded by Matthew, the ones who were productive received more money. In Luke the productive servants were given more responsibility. The ones who returned ten times as much were put in charge of ten cities. The one who returned five times as much was put in charge of five cities.

In both stories the unproductive servants had the money taken from them. Jesus is like any good leader who expects his followers to participate in the cause. Doing nothing is not something the King of Kings appreciates.

Jesus Accounts for Individual Differences

Another effective leadership practice is to take into account individual differences. Jesus loved Peter and John equally, but he treated them differently. As a result of Peter's hasty decisions, Jesus corrected Peter often, but Jesus also rewarded Peter for his willingness to exercise his faith. Jesus worked with Peter diligently to help him develop into an effective leader of the church. Jesus took John under his wing and was gentler with him. John was able to witness some of Jesus' caring—benevolent acts which others may not have known about—such as keeping the managers of the wedding at Cana from embarrassment and Jesus' willingness to forgive as He suffered on the cross.

Matthew may seem like a strange choice for an apostle—even more peculiar than the rest. He was a tax collector, more loathed by the

Jews than Americans dislike the Internal Revenue Service. He had to give detailed accounting to the Romans. I agree with the Catholics that Matthew at least started his gospel before the other disciples. (The finishing touches may not have been put in until after Mark finished his gospel, likely based on interviews with Peter). Matthew provided a meticulously detailed account of the public teachings of Jesus, who would have had an opportunity to review what Matthew recorded for accuracy, as well as stoke Matthew's interest in Old Testament prophecies about the Messiah.

During his 3½ year ministry, Jesus healed hundreds of people in individual encounters. The Christian emphasis on individuals runs so deep in the American conscious that socialists have had an uphill battle in trying to promote groupthink consensus—failing to gain converts despite propagating unrealistic expectations of comfortable wealth with little effort. No one put a bigger dent in class envy than Jesus, the greatest advocate for loving our individual neighbors.

Jesus, Our Example

Jesus was, is and will be a great role model of civil leadership. In his first letter, the Apostle Peter said Jesus left us with an example that we should follow in His steps (1Peter 2:21). The Apostle John recorded that Jesus told His disciples to love each other as he had loved them (John 15:13). Jesus inspired people to follow Him because He sacrificed for them. Jesus showed His love for us in that while we were sinners, He died for us (Romans 5:8). Although Jesus was sinless, He took the penalty for us so that God could be both just and merciful. While we will not accomplish it with the same expertise as our example, we are also to be just and merciful. The Apostle Paul said that those who heard him should follow him as he followed Christ (1 Corinthians 11:1). To Timothy, Paul said Christ Jesus came into the world to save sinners of whom he was the worst. In showing mercy Jesus displayed His unlimited patience as an example to those who would believe in Him and receive eternal life

(1 Timothy 1:12-17). Timothy was to set an example for believers in speech, in life, in love, in faith and purity (1 Timothy 4:12). Following the example of Jesus, Paul told Timothy to entrust the mission to reliable men who would be qualified to teach others.

When I was at Colorado State University, I was part of the Navigators who tried to implement the Great Commission. That commission was to intensely teach others who would grow into disciples, who would disciple others, who would in turn disciple others, and so on. We met to pray, study the Bible, and make specific plans to share the gospel so that fellow students would have opportunities to receive Jesus as their Savior and Lord. One Nav leader posed a question, "Should we try to change individuals in order to change society, or should we try to change society in order to change individuals?" His answer at the time was to work on changing individuals. My belated answer is to work on both. Jesus wants us to work on transforming individuals and nations.

Jesus Teaches Us to Think Critically

Jesus told His disciples He would no longer call them servants because a servant does not know his master's business (John 15:14-15). Jesus has taught His disciples so they can know that their business is to love God and love others. People do not automatically become friends of God. We need to recognize that God is God, and we are not. Those who receive Jesus are given the power to become children of God. We will never become the Father, but we will mature into adult believers who understand God's purposes and carry them out as He provides the strength, for without Him we can do nothing (John 15:5). Jesus commands us to love God with all our heart, soul, and mind and to love others as He loved. To love means to want the best for those we love. That requires careful thought.

The Kingdom of God will partly be defined by who will not be there. In John's vision he saw an angel coming down from heaven having the key to the abyss and a great chain in his hand. He bound the devil for a thousand years and threw him into the abyss so that he would not deceive the nations any longer until the end of the thousand years (Revelation 20: 1-3). The millennial kingdom will be noted for an absence of deception and a proliferation of delightful truth.

The truth will give our minds peace. We do not realize the extent to which deception makes it hellish on earth. Nor do we appreciate how much a proliferation of truth is going to make it like heaven. When we perceive the truth that we have a Creator, God reveals more truth to us. When people reject the Creator, God gives them over to a depraved mind (Romans 1:28). God uses the devil to give people alternatives if they do not want to follow Christ. If at the beginning of the millennium, the devil is removed, and Christ is the focus of government, then there will be a widespread peace that will ease troubled minds.

One of the great paradoxes of life is that seeking one's own way leads to slavery to sin and obedience to God leads to freedom. The devil distracts people from that truth and at times outright contradicts it by telling people, like he did Eve, that God is holding out on them. Contrary to what the devil says, wanting people to avoid the tragic consequences of sin is not exactly holding out on them.

"Conflict is inevitable, but combat is optional. Use your God-given creative energy to solve conflict before it escalates into combat. Perhaps the seeds of kindness will not sprout for a long time, so get started now" (Lucado, 1995).

Those who reign with the Prince of Peace during the millennium will have a great opportunity for peace of mind. Individuals at peace with God and at peace with themselves will be at peace with each other. In ancient times of war, men would construct swords and spears. In times of peace, they would use a hammer to reshape their swords into the metal part of plows, and they would fashion their spears into pruning hooks. During the thousand years characterized by peace, perhaps factories that once constructed weapons will instead manufacture agricultural equipment and those who plant vineyards will eat their fruit.

The peace on earth and good will toward mem will extend to how we treat animals. We will treat them well. When animals left the ark God made them afraid of humans and humans feared the more ferocious animals. In the Messianic kingdom, the lion and the calf will lie down together and a young child shall play in the midst of snakes (Isaiah 11:6). Caregivers will not fear for their children's safety from wild creatures. They will not even have to be afraid of snakes. The paintings of a lion, lamb and child give a vision of the coming kingdom. Jesus is both the Lamb who takes away the sin of the world and the Lion who will establish justice on the earth. Jesus encourages children to come to Him.

Jesus will govern with righteousness. His knowledge of the truth will help Him to make sound judgements. Jesus told His disciples to love, and He demonstrated love by His example. To love means to do the best for. Jesus will make decisions that will account for the poor and needy (Isaiah 11:4). The fairness of His leadership will contribute to peace. People who make heaven heavenly will tend to accept righteous decisions.

Jesus Presents His Followers with a Vision and a Mission

First and foremost, the Kingdom of God will be defined by the presence of Jesus who is the source of love, peace and joy. The Kingdom of God is wherever God governs. God rules in heaven and He rules in the hearts of those who accept His program of blessing. God's plan to mature His followers includes the establishment of the Kingdom of God. Through numerous parables, Jesus presented us with a vision of the Kingdom of God. When Jesus physically returns to the earth, His followers will help Him rule over the whole earth. Representatives from nations will show their respect for Him.

During the millennium, Jesus will govern along with those who will be given authority to judge. When the mother of John and

Andrew asked Jesus if her sons could sit on either side of Him when He established His Kingdom. Jesus did not deny that He would have lieutenants at His side, but He said those who would be there would be revealed later. The twelve disciples will govern the twelve tribes of Israel during the thousand years.

Jesus will counsel those in leadership positions on how to govern. His loving personality is going to be wonderful to be near for those who have received His righteousness. He will be like a father to His children, always seeking to give them what they need and want. Jesus teaches His disciples to be servants. When leaders are also servants we approach Heaven.

Beginning with Adam and Eve, God's purpose for mankind has been to be fruitful and multiply. That purpose continues in our age since Christ's first advent. Beginning with Jesus' first ministry, God's purpose for those who choose Him is to be born again. When Jesus returns, there will be no more marriage in that age for procreation, but there will be opportunities for people to be born again.

In Luke 20:34-36 Jesus says the people of this age marry and are given in marriage. But in the resurrection and age to come there will be no marriage. In reference to the Messianic Kingdom, Isaiah says that people will live much longer. In the kingdom to come infants may be brought back to life and given a lengthy opportunity to accept or reject Christ. It seems crazy that anyone would rebel against Christ, but Revelation says the rebellious will be numerous like the sand on the seashore.

People tend to think that when they die, they will go to heaven and that's it. They think we will be in a static bliss without any challenges. However, when believers die, we will go to be with Jesus, and we will be with Him forever. That means that we will return to Earth when Jesus returns. By means of faith I know that my redeemer lives and He on the Earth again will stand. By faith I know that I will reign with Him.

At the end of the millennium, God will sit on a Great White Throne and judge people according to their deeds. Those who have been deceived will not be a part of the New Heaven: neither the sexually immoral, nor idolaters, nor adulterers, nor male prostitutes, nor homosexual offenders, nor thieves, nor the greedy, nor drunkards, nor slanderers, nor swindlers. When we call for repentance, we are not being hateful, rather we are seeking their own good, because in this life repentance will be met with reconciliation. Some of the people Paul was writing to had repented and become a part of the church which is in the kingdom of God (1 Corinthians 6:9-11).

All the rebellious against God will be removed. Only those who obey God will remain with Him so that heaven can be heavenly. The millennium will be a step toward Heaven from the way things are now, but there will still be some suffering and death. In the coming New Heaven after the millennium, there will be no more tears and no more pain. We will delight in the presence of the One who sacrificed so much for us to be with God.

Jesus left us with a mission. He said, "All authority has been given to Me in heaven and on earth. Go therefore and make disciples of all the nations, baptizing them in the name of the Father and the Son and the Holy Spirit, teaching them to observe all that I commanded you; and lo, I am with you always, even to the end of the age" (Matthew 28:18-20). We are to bring individuals to Christ and teach them what Jesus taught. We are also to have a role in encouraging national governments to freely let us be witnesses of our relationships with God.

"You shall receive power when the Holy Spirit has come upon you; and you shall be my witnesses both in Jerusalem, and in all Judea and Samaria, and even to the remotest part of the earth" (Acts 1:8).

Both Daniel 7:18 and Revelation 22:5 say that saints will reign throughout the ages forever. Heaven will be governed civilly. Now we have a choice in America of whether we want to approach a heavenly government or if we will go on harming one another.

America, choose civility.

Jesus and Civil Leadership

Vision/Mission – Kingdom of God/Share the Good News throughout the world
Think critically – Be friends of God, ruling with love
Be an example – Sacrifice to benefit others
Consider individual differences – Always
Expect meaningful participation – Including all God-given talents and responsibilities
Supply needs for ministry – Jesus enables us to do all things required
Jesus will establish a just society – Where people will thrive in His Love

References

Scripture references are mostly from my paraphrases of cited Bible passages. Any Biblical references not shown in quotation marks are my paraphrases. I feel comfortable paraphrasing since I studied Greek at Southwestern Baptist Theological Seminary and Golden Gate Baptist Theological Seminary, and I studied Hebrew at Golden Gate Baptist Theological Seminary. Unless otherwise noted, scripture shown in quotation marks is from the 1995 Translation of the New American Standard Bible, published by Zondervan, Grand Rapids, Michigan. www.zondervan.com. Where applicable, I reference as sources either KJV King James Version or NIV New

International Version, copyright held by The Lockman Foundation, LaHabra, California. www.Lockman.org

Adams, J.Q. (1837). *Independence Day Speech.* Teaching American History: A Project of the Ashland Center at Ashland University.

Alinsky, S. (1989). *Rules for radicals: A practical primer for realistic radicals.* Random House.

AZAG. (2019) Arizona man sentenced two years' probation for voter fraud. Arizona Attorney General. October 3, 2019.

Bandura, A. (1977). *Social learning theory.* Upper Saddle River, NJ: Prentice Hall.

Barton, D. (2008). *Original intent, the courts, the Constitution, & religion.* Wallbuilders Press.

Bass, B.M. (1998). *Transformational leadership: Industrial, military, and educational impact.* Mahwah, NJ: Lawrence Erlbaum Associates.

Bossie, D. (2022). *Mark Zuckerberg learns the hard way that politics is a full-contact sport.* Posted by David Bossie of Citizens United in the *Washington Times;* updated 11/1/2022.

Brown University. (2013). *Costs of War.* Watson Institute of International Studies.

Byrd, J.P. (2017). *Sacred Scripture, Sacred War: The Bible and the American Revolution.* Reprint Oxford University Press. ISBN-0190697563.

Burns, J.M. (1978). *Leadership.* New York, New York: Harper & Row.

Calvin, J. (2022). *DNC, Clinton Campaign agree to Steele dossier funding fine.* New York: Associated Press. March 31, 2022.

Campbell, D. & Stanley. (1963). *Experimental and quasi-experimental designs for research.* Chicago, IL: Rand McNally.

Chalkbeat. (2022). Retrieved from: co.chalkbeat.org.

Condra, B. (2019). *The insanity of incivility and what can be done about it.* Self-published, available on Amazon.

Cummings, W. (2018). *USA Today,* October 9. Retrieved from: usatoday.com

Davidson, J.D. (2025). What we know and what we don't about January 6, Imprimis 311, imprimis.hillsdale.edu

Drayer, D. (2016). Socratic.org.

Dwyer, R. (2012). ADST Association for Diplomatic Studies and Training.

Estapa, J. (2009). *The relationship between the transformational leadership characteristics of principals as perceived by teachers, and student achievement on standardized tests.* (Doctoral dissertation). ProQuest. (UMI Number 3378413).

Flashoff, J. & Snow, R. (1970). *A case study in statistical inference: Reconsideration of the Rosenthal-Jacobson data on teacher expectancy.* U.S. Office of Education. ERIC ED046892.

Heisenberg, Werner (1930). *The Physical Principles of the Quantum Theory.* Dover Publications. Translated by Carl Eckart & F.C. Hoyt. From lectures given at the University of Chicago in 1927.

History.com. Editors. (2018). *Inquisition.* Published by A & E Television Networks.

Hogan, W.C. (2007). *Many minds, one heart: Dream for a new America.* The University of North Carolina Press.

Keeling, C. and Piper, S. (2001). *Exchanges of atmospheric CO_2 and $^{13}CO_2$ with the terrestrial biosphere and oceans from 1978 to 2000. IV, critical overview.* 510 Reference Series, No. 01-09 (Revised from 510 Reference Series, No. 00-24.) Scripps Institution of Oceanography, San Diego. Pp. 1-17.

Jefferson, T. (1816). *Letter from Thomas Jefferson to Isaac Tiffany.* Founders

Online. Downloaded 4/25/2020.

Kennedy, J. (1961). *Inaugural address.* JFK Library.

Leithwood, J. & Jantzi, D. (1997). Explaining variation in teacher's perceptions of principal's leadership: A replication. *Journal of Educational Administration,* 35(4), 312-331. Retrieved from ProQuest.

Lemov, D. (2010). *Teach like a champion: Techniques that put students on the path to college (1st ed.).* San Francisco: Jossey-Bass. ISBN 978-1119712619.

Lucado, M. (1995). *Life lessons from the inspired word of God.* The Inspirational Study Bible. Word Publishing. ISBN 978-08499-5123-7.

Madison, J. (1787). *Federalist No. 10.* Bill of Rights Institute.

Mann, J. (2020). *The great rift: Dick Cheney, Colin Powell, and the broken friendship that defined an era,* Henry Holt and Co. ISBN 978-1627797559.

Machiavelli, N. (1532). *The Prince.* Translated by George Bull and published by Penguin Classics in 2003.

Mayo Clinic. (2025). *Drugs and Supplements.* mayoclinic.org viewed 6/25/2025.

NCES. (2021). National Center for Educational Statistics. Retrieved from: nces.ed.gov.

National Archives. (1776). *Declaration of Independence: A Transcription.*

National Archives. (1789). *The Bill of Rights: A Transcription.*

Nunes, D. (2020). *Countdown to socialism.* Encounter Books.

Obama, B. (2020). *A Promised Land.* New York, NY: Crown.

Ochieng, N., Chidambaram, P., Garfield, R., Neuman, T. (2021). *Factors associated with COVID-19 cases and deaths in long-term care facilities: Findings from a literature review.* Kaiser Family Foundation.

Phillips, K. (2018). *Heidi Heitkamp calls out Hillary Clinton for saying Democrats cannot be civil with Republicans.'* Washingtonpost.com/politics/2018/10/10.

Prater, M.E. (2004). *The relative impact of principal managerial, instructional, and transformational leadership on student achievement* (Doctoral dissertation). Retrieved from ProQuest. (UMI Number 3206343).

PBS. (2021). *Pence's full letter saying he can't claim 'unilateral authority' to reject electoral votes.* Public Broadcasting System. pbs.org (1/6/2021).

Reynolds E. (5/7/2019) Fox Business.

Rosenthal, R. & Jacobson, L. (1968). *Pygmalion in the classroom: Teacher expectations and pupil's intellectual development.* New York, NY: Holt, Rinehart, & Winston.

Saxe, J.G. (1873). Family Friendly Poems.

Schurz, C. (1858).

Skinner, B. (1971). *Beyond freedom & dignity.* New York, NY: Alfred A. Knoph.

Smithsonian. (2020). *A brief history of the Salem Witch Trials.* Smithsonian Magazine.

Swaine, J. & Brown, E. (2022). *Sidney Powell's nonprofit raised $16 million as she spread election falsehoods.* Washington Post (10/14/2022).

Werner, R.M., Hoffman, J.D., & Coe, N.B. (2020). *Long-term care policy after Covid-19: Solving the nursing home crisis.* The New England Journal of Medicine.

Wise, J. (5/7/2019). *The Hill*; thehill.com

Woodbrey, A. (2022). *District Attorney investigation finds no evidence of criminal election activity.*

About the Author

Dr. Wayne Wolf is an academic manager with Job Corps. A former Delta County Commissioner, he has experience in leadership and administration in agriculture, business, non-profits, and government. He earned a Ph.D. in Public Policy and Administration from Walden University. His research expertise focuses on transformational and civil leadership. His master's degree emphasized curriculum development and the art of dealing with difficult students. He taught leadership, ethics, and public administration courses at Colorado Christian University. His wife, Kristine, has worked with Wayne on the family ranch, mission projects and political campaigns.

www.ingramcontent.com/pod-product-compliance
Lightning Source LLC
Chambersburg PA
CBHW052105230426
43671CB00011B/1936